A Century of Female Revolution

A Century of Female Revolution

From Peterloo to Parliament

Glynis Cooper

PEN & SWORD
HISTORY

AN IMPRINT OF PEN & SWORD BOOKS LTD.
YORKSHIRE – PHILADELPHIA

First published in Great Britain in 2020 by
Pen & Sword History
An imprint of
Pen & Sword Books Ltd
Yorkshire – Philadelphia

Copyright © Glynis Cooper, 2020

ISBN 978 1 52673 921 6

The right of Glynis Cooper to be identified as the Author of this work has been asserted by her in accordance with the Copyright, Designs and Patents Act 1988.

A CIP catalogue record for this book is available from the British Library.

Printed and bound in England
By TJ Books, Padstow, Cornwall

Pen & Sword Books Ltd incorporates the Imprints of Pen & Sword Archaeology, Atlas, Aviation, Battleground, Discovery, Family History, History, Maritime, Military, Naval, Politics, Railways, Select, Transport, True Crime, Fiction, Frontline Books, Leo Cooper, Praetorian Press, Seaforth Publishing, Wharncliffe and White Owl.

For a complete list of Pen & Sword titles please contact

PEN & SWORD BOOKS LIMITED
47 Church Street, Barnsley, South Yorkshire, S70 2AS, England
E-mail: enquiries@pen-and-sword.co.uk
Website: www.pen-and-sword.co.uk

or

PEN AND SWORD BOOKS
1950 Lawrence Rd, Havertown, PA 19083, USA
E-mail: uspen-and-sword@casematepublishers.com
Website: www.penandswordbooks.com

Dedication

'Never forget. You are a person too.'
(Stan Barstow to Glynis Cooper c.1979)

Dedicated to all females who fought so long and hard
for fair democracy, social justice, and women's rights,
especially the thousands of unknown and unsung heroines
of history who helped to rewrite the pages of destiny for
so many women they would never know.

Acknowledgements

Grateful thanks are due to Michael Wood for the introduction, to the British Newspaper Library, Manchester Central Library, John Rylands University Library, Chetham's Library, Oldham Municipal Library, People's History Museum, Manchester Histories, to members of the Peterloo Project, to Mike Greenman for being a 'Peterloo Laurel', to Amy Jordan and Heather Williams at Pen & Sword, to all the proof readers, editors, designers, and publishers who made this book a reality, and to family and friends as ever.

Contents

Foreword

This fascinating book tells an untold story; how the Peterloo Massacre in 1819 lit the fuse for ordinary working women's fight for representation, which continued through the Chartists up to the Suffragettes and the winning of the vote in 1919. It's the tale of the heroines who fought the hundred-year battle for women's rights and universal suffrage.

The setting is the Manchester region and the inciting incident of the story is Peterloo, that key moment in the history of British democracy when the English state unleashed deadly violence on its own citizens. On 16 August 1819 a 60,000 strong demonstration for parliamentary reform, gathered in a Wakes Week atmosphere in St Peter's Fields, was attacked by regular troops and local yeomanry. Eighteen were killed and 700 injured. New research using Home Office records and letters shows the authorities had decided in advance to use force to disperse the crowd.

Such shocking violence aroused almost universal outrage. The massacre provoked a torrent of great journalism; many radical papers sprang up, and the *Manchester Guardian* was founded in the aftermath. The outpouring of songs and poetry included Shelley's *Masque of Anarchy*, perhaps our greatest political poem. 'The magistrates and yeomanry were defending a corrupt system,' wrote the historian A.J.P. Taylor. 'The demonstrators were demanding their just rights. They spoke for the people of England.'

The story of Peterloo is especially vivid to all in the North-West where it lived long in popular memory. I remember on my first day at Manchester Grammar School, aged 11, our history teacher Ian Bailey reminded us that our home town was 'the city of the Industrial

Revolution, the Chartists and Suffragettes', but also 'the city of the heroes – *and the heroines* – of Peterloo, and boys don't you forget it!'. (Indeed a well-known study of the massacre written on the hundredth anniversary was written by a master at MGS, Francis Bruton).

There were heroines too. We might not have realised it when we were young, because for we baby-boomer boys, heroes tended to be men. But nonetheless we were aware, even as children listening to our parents and aunts and neighbours, what a big role women had played in the World Wars. Now, in Glynis' book, we can see what a role they played throughout our history. At Peterloo women figuring disproportionately in the casualty lists, many depicted in contemporary cartoons and engravings in their Sunday best white dresses and caps, being savagely attacked by mounted troops wielding sabres. The testimonies of the women who met the full force of the cavalry charge form one of the most striking and moving sections of Glynis' book. One of them was Mary Fildes, the Irish-born first president of the Manchester Female Reform Society, who was seriously wounded. Mary is portrayed in one of the most famous images of the day, a coloured engraving whose caption says it is 'dedicated to Henry Hunt and the female reformers of Manchester and the adjacent towns who were exposed to and suffered from the wanton and fiendish attack....' On her banner we can read the words 'Manchester Female Reform Society', although as she later recalled its main message was 'Let us die like men and not be sold like slaves.'

Glynis' book is an object lesson in forgotten histories: what was deliberately concealed; what has been lost; what can still be retrieved by patient delving, as Glynis has done. To give a personal example, let me focus on the photograph of Failsworth Peterloo veterans, which she has described in her book. My father was born in Failsworth, from which a sizeable contingent went to Peterloo. Recently my sister started doing our family tree, and traced the Woods in Failsworth in an unbroken line back to the eighteenth century. Dad's grandfather, Jim, had agitated for voting reform in the 1860s, and raised money for victims of the 1860s Cotton Famine. They had friends and relatives at Peterloo, like the Schofields and the Kershaws.

But it was only after my mother died in summer 2016, aged nearly 97, that I discovered the full significance of these facts. Clearing out her house, we opened a box of my dad's bits and pieces, among which was a bundle of photos, postcards and books about his native place: a guide to Failsworth, a pamphlet by the local poet Ben Brierley, a tatty booklet about the famous Failsworth Pole, which had been erected in 1793 by the village 'Tories' against the 'Jacobins', the radicals who were fighting for reform and who had organised for the 1819 demonstration. It was at the Pole (which still stands, though now a brick clock tower) that the demonstrators had gathered before marching to Peterloo, crowning their leaders with the French 'Cap of Liberty'. The huge crowd included women's groups from Oldham and surrounding villages, and twenty-four young women from Failsworth led the way, crowning the leaders of the Oldham contingent. The place had been violently split on party lines; the librarian of the radical library on the green by the Pole (where a bronze statue of Brierley now stands) was attacked for having a copy of Tom Paine's *Rights of Man*; returning wounded were mocked and abused by their opponents. But they didn't lose their nerve. After Peterloo local people raised funds for Richard Carlile, the radical publisher who had been on the platform at Peterloo, but was then in Dorchester Gaol. Their letter was signed by fifty Failsworth men and women, readers of Paine, free thinkers, atheists and republicans; an extraordinary insight into the culture of these Lancashire mill towns, which was noted by national writers such as William Cobbett; a culture which was also shared by the women.

What Glynis also shows so clearly is that the build up to the hot summer of 1819 was a crucial moment of change for women across the region and the wider country. At this point women's reform associations were founded in Manchester, Royden, Saddleworth, Blackburn, Stockport, Oldham, Rochdale and elsewhere. I wonder too if some of these movements had earlier roots? The genealogy of women's protest and political action includes major eighteenth century writers like Anna Laetitia Barbauld and Mary Wollstonecraft, but further back one suspects there are many still untraced links to the seventeenth-century radical movements and when women radicals like Kathleen Chidley organised her 1649 'Humble Petition of divers well-affected women'. 'Have we not an interest with the men of this Nation?' Chidley wrote, raising 6,000 women's signatures opposing the trial of John Lilburne in 1653. Even further back, women had been prominent in the Lollard movement which, in the nineteenth-century local legend, was connected with Failsworth. If only we knew more, then, about the secret history of women's education and reading in the decades before Peterloo, when, as E.P. Thomson showed in his famous book *The Making of the English Working Class*, a new people's culture arose, in which women played a significant role.

This tradition of women's radicalism came to a head in the turbulent and troubled years after Waterloo. In 1818 Sam Bamford attended a big reform meeting at Saddleworth where, for the first time in his experience, the women voted. 'From that time,' he said, 'women voted with men at radical meetings' (a story Glynis tells on page 9). This gave a major new impetus to grass roots political movements, as Bamford himself saw; it is a key moment in the story of women's rights in Britain. At Peterloo, women's groups from Manchester, Oldham, Rochdale, and Blackburn carried the banners of female reform societies, many of them formed in that electric summer of 1819. History, we might say, was on the move.

At Peterloo the presence of women is also illustrated by the extraordinary photograph of Peterloo veterans, which Glynis discusses (page 100). This unique image was taken by a weaving shed in Wrigley Head, Failsworth, on 27 September 1884, sixty-five years after the massacre. It shows eleven Failsworth Peterloo veterans, most then in their eighties. They were still fighting for the franchise and they attended the Great Reform Demonstration that day, displaying a tattered and faded banner that they had carried in 1819 showing the word 'Liberty'. Some of them, the Schofields, Whitakers, Chaddertons and Ogdens, were old Failsworth families who had lived there since the 1650s. Among them were three women, Susan Whitaker, Mary Collins and Catherine McMurdo; all hale and hearty as they posed by the loom shed near the Anglers Arms (where my great-great-grandmother, Hannah, a former bobbin winder, was landlady).

That day in 1884 they told stories, the women lighting their long 'bacca' pipes. Mary Collins sang a fifteen-verse Peterloo ballad by an Ashton weaver, John Stafford, who had been at the massacre, and their stories vividly brought back the horror and shock of that sparkling blue summer day in St Peters Fields – miraculously preserved in the pages of the *Oldham Weekly Chronicle*, whose riveting account Glynis reproduces in the book.

As a glimpse of that extraordinary event, sixty-five years on, and as an insight into a forgotten people's history – and women's history – I find this an incredibly moving image. All of which goes to show that our rights in an open democratic society with freedom of speech and a free press, were never simply given benevolently by the rich and powerful, but were struggled for by ordinary men and women, often at great sacrifice to themselves. And that is the real story of Glynis' book. Were the veterans in the photograph alive today, they would no doubt be on the march again, carrying their banner for liberty. The struggle goes on!

Michael Wood, 2020

Preface

It is difficult to assess what elements of nineteenth-century life were a result of Peterloo and which were complementary to the main event. There were so many facets to Peterloo, and so many ultimate achievements of its aims which overlapped into areas not originally foreseen. For example, were the Public Health Acts of the 1870s or the Education Acts of the 1870s and 1880s a direct result of Peterloo? The whole of the nineteenth century was a time of great change. Initially it was the advance of the Industrial Revolution which caused changes, but Peterloo encapsulated the struggle of adaptation. For centuries there had been a wealthy landed 'upper order' of limited numbers and a 'lower order' of 'the masses', generally despised by the 'upper orders', but who nevertheless needed their labour in order to maintain their own comfortable lifestyles. Poverty was rampant, both in urban and industrial areas. Not unnaturally, those forced to live in poverty wanted something better. Not unnaturally, those who had had privileged lifestyles did not wish to sacrifice them. It is a problem which still affects much of the world today. Back in pre-history, before 'class' was invented, the first person to work out how to make fire for warmth and cooking, the first person to invent the wheel, the first people to weave or sew clothing, were just ordinary people, and may well have been women. Stone Age farmers lived in small settlements with dwellings of equal size. There were farmers, bakers, butchers, basket makers, potters and tool makers, but they were all obviously regarded as equally important to an interdependent society. There was also a system of social care. People with illness or disability lived to ages far beyond those at which they would have died had it not been for carers. That much is discernible from the archaeological record; but all this appeared to change when precious metals were first discovered, and suddenly settlements evolve into one large dwelling surrounded by a few hovels. Some burials are grander. Grave goods (precious objects a person might need for the next life) became more exotic. From that time, subsequent divisions between the groups of 'haves' and 'have-nots' have persisted right down to the present day and throughout the centuries have caused grief, suffering, problems, uprisings and wars. Peterloo was just such an event. Initially a peaceful protest, it turned into a nightmare of violence and carnage but that was only the beginning.

Chapter 1

Background to Peterloo

In the early nineteenth century, despite the growth of the cotton industry, Manchester's burgeoning population was not represented at all in Parliament, nor were Stockport or Saddleworth, although the government was very happy to acquire the wealth and profits being generated by 'Cottonopolis'. At the same time, although Manchester did not have any parliamentary representation, there were 'rotten boroughs', deserted villages. Each of them could return two members of parliament who were usually local landed gentry. Thus, a comparatively tiny number could wield disproportionate power, so there was a crucial and pressing need for electoral reform. Old Sarum in Wiltshire, which had no inhabitants at all, and Dunwich in Suffolk, which had disappeared into the sea, are probably the best-known examples of rotten boroughs. Only a tiny percentage of the male population had a vote, and many of these voters did not have a choice for whom they voted. There were also property qualifications which were necessary before anyone could stand for Parliament, reducing the availability of those who wanted to be electoral candidates. The basis of the three main political demands of the workers were: that one MP should represent each constituency, each constituency should be of equal size and that there should be universal suffrage.

Although there had been some talk of votes for women, universal suffrage would be intended for male voters only at this time. It was felt that once all men had the vote, votes for women might follow. Electoral reform was long overdue, but not unnaturally, this was fiercely resisted by the elite and entitled upper classes. The other main grievance at this time was the Corn Laws, introduced to maintain a high price for corn after the Napoleonic wars, so that the aristocracy could make handsome profits by keeping bread prices high. Repeal of the Corn Laws had become essential if everyone was to be able to afford to eat. Britain was producing goods at extremely low prices to the advantage of both home and foreign consumers. However, one million people employed in cotton manufacturing did not have the means of becoming consumers to half the extent they could have done if a minimum price for weaving was fixed. It was felt that both workers and manufacturers should have 'wholesome regulations' on weaving prices. As it was, over production resulted in under trading and weavers were laid off because their employers could not afford to pay them. Most weavers were either on part-time work or had no employment at all. Folk were struggling to feed themselves and their families, and to keep a roof over their heads, but protests went unheeded because they had no official voice in Parliament and therefore no say in government or legislation.

There was no social security system, just the hated Poor Laws, which meant that if folk couldn't support themselves, they would end up a pauper in the workhouse, where conditions were spartan and the unremitting menial chores hard and repetitive. It was a fate many dreaded. Out of this situation was born the need and desire for urgent reform to alleviate the hunger and suffering of those with no work, and those working long hours for low wages. Reform movements grew, asking for a democratic parliamentary system to be established, and the means to earn a fair day's pay for a fair day's work. There had been unrest about the dire economic situation for some time. The cost of the Napoleonic Wars caused economic hardship in Britain and wages had fallen sharply in the northern towns of Cottonopolis. Even before the battle of Waterloo (15 June 1815) there had been poverty, distress and much resentment of how working-class people were treated which, in turn, had led to radical outlooks and the formation of radical clubs. In 1812, the year of Napoleon's retreat from Moscow, Major John Cartwright had formed the first Hampden Club in London. His brother was Edmund Cartwright who had designed and built the power loom in the mid-1770s; this may have influenced John Cartwright's ideas as much as it influenced radical thought in northern industrial cities. These clubs aimed to bring together more moderate members of the middle classes with radical working-class people.

The first Hampden Club outside London was formed in 1816 at Royden on the Wirral by William Fitton. This was followed by a rash of Hampden Clubs in the Manchester area including: Middleton Hampden Club, formed by Samuel Bamford; Oldham Hampden Club, formed by Joseph Healey; Manchester Hampden Club, formed by John Knight and Joseph Johnson. The authorities were wary of these clubs and arrested John Knight in 1813 to make the point. Nevertheless he persisted in his beliefs that there should be universal suffrage, a secret ballot and annual parliaments. Initially, however, his efforts were constantly thwarted by endless arguments over how much property a potential voter should own. His idea was that universal suffrage should mean just that. All men should be entitled to a vote whatever their financial or property-owning status. For the most part, women were not generally included in the concept of universal suffrage at this time. There were also clubs in Rochdale, Ashton-under-Lyne and Stockport. Political issues were debated and radical newspapers, like the *Manchester Observer* and *Black Dwarf* were read.

1815 was not a good year, especially for the working classes. The Corn Laws had been introduced that year to protect the landed gentry against cheaper foreign imports of grain, but this had only served to increase the price of grain by decreasing the supplies, which was causing severe problems for the poor.

In 1813, a House of Commons Committee had recommended excluding foreign-grown corn until the price of domestically grown corn increased to 80 shillings (£4 – equivalent to £260 in 2018) per quarter (8 bushels): or currently equivalent to around £1,102 per tonne of wheat.

Augustus de Morgan, 1830

There were a number of reasons for this and they were neatly summed up by historian Asa Briggs (1959).

> First, it would guarantee the prosperity of the manufacturer by affording him outlets for his products. Second, it would relieve the Condition of England question by cheapening the price of food and ensuring more regular employment. Third, it would make English agriculture more efficient by stimulating demand for its products in urban and industrial areas. Fourth, it would introduce through mutually advantageous international trade a new era of international fellowship and peace. The only barrier to these four beneficent solutions was the ignorant self-interest of the landlords, the 'bread-taxing oligarchy, unprincipled, unfeeling, rapacious and plundering'.

What could possibly go wrong?

In April 1815 there was a huge volcanic eruption of Mount Tambora in Indonesia which caused extreme weather conditions worldwide, followed by 'the year without a summer' in 1816 when thick fog covered the land for months; there were severe frosts, heavy rain fell in the summer months and temperatures dropped catastrophically. The harvests were ruined and there was widespread famine. Although there was some improvement by 1817, it was not enough to remedy the food situation and most workers were desperate. However, the basic problem was that the price of bread was rising at the same time as manufacturers were cutting wages. Richard Cobden (co-founder with John Bright of the Anti-Corn Law League in 1838) praised the following speech made by a hard-pressed working-class man.

> When provisions are high, the people have so much to pay for them that they have little or nothing left to buy clothes with; and when they have little to buy clothes with, there are few clothes sold; and when there are few clothes sold, there are

too many to sell, they are very cheap; and when they are very cheap, there cannot be much paid for making them: and that, consequently, the manufacturing working man's wages are reduced, the mills are shut up, business is ruined, and general distress is spread through the country. But when, as now, the working man has the said 25s left in his pocket, he buys more clothing with it (ay, and other articles of comfort too), and that increases the demand for them, and the greater the demand … makes them rise in price, and the rising price enables the working man to get higher wages and the masters better profits. This, therefore, is the way I prove that high provisions make lower wages, and cheap provisions make higher wages.

Bright and Thorold Rogers

The year was overshadowed by the death in childbirth of Princess Charlotte, the only legitimate child of the Prince Regent. The baby was a boy, but he was stillborn. Princess Charlotte was popular, and her death highlighted yet again the dangers of childbirth. At the beginning of 1817, Thomas Wooler, a London-based journalist, founded a new radical journal named *Black Dwarf*. It became a successful publication which was supported by Sir John Cartwright, who had founded the Hampden Clubs, which were, in turn, supported by *Black Dwarf*. Wooler compared the Hampden Clubs to the Quakers.

Those who condemn clubs either do not understand what they can accomplish, or they wish nothing to be done … Let us look at, and emulate, the patient resolution of the Quakers. They have conquered without arms – without violence – without threats. They conquered by union.

Wooler was arrested on charges of 'seditious libel' in May 1817, but was acquitted. Like many before him and after him, Wooler argued that the real culprit was capitalism.

Let him abandon the labourer to his own protection; cease to oppress him, and the poor man would scorn to hold any fictitious dependence upon the rich. Give him a fair price for his labour, and do not take two-thirds of a depreciated remuneration back from him again in the shape of taxes. Lower the extravagance of the great. Tax those real luxuries, enormous fortunes obtained without merit. Reduce the herd of locusts that prey upon the honey of the hive, and think they do the bees a most essential service by robbing them. The working bee can always find a hive. Do not take from them what they can earn, to supply the wants of those who will earn nothing. Do this; and the poor will not want your splendid erections for the cultivation of misery and the subjugation of the mind.

Early in 1817 an electoral reform bill had been drafted by workers and there were meetings held in Manchester with a view to petitioning the Crown directly for reform and relief. However, in January 1817, the Prince Regent's coach had been attacked by rioting London workers. Consequently, the Prince Regent was not in a receptive frame of mind and this resulted in the passing of the Treason Act 1817 and the Seditious Meetings Act 1817, engineered by Lord Sidmouth and known as the 'Gagging Acts'. Habeas Corpus was suspended for fourteen months (January 1817 – March 1818); meetings of over fifty people were banned, and magistrates could arrest anyone suspected of 'seditious libel'. As a result, there were vitriolic attacks upon those whom the Establishment saw as 'the scum of the earth'. Consequently, there were several uprisings around the country, notably in Stockport, Leicester, Birmingham, London Smithfield and at Pentridge in Nottingham. There were also a couple of 'Blanket Marches', one in March 1817 composed of Manchester workers, and another in the autumn of 1818 composed of both male and female weavers from Manchester, Stockport and Ashton-under-Lyne. Both were organised in Manchester. The idea was that thousands of workers should march to London to protest about lack of jobs, enforced starvation and to demand a right to vote so that they had some say in how the country was run. The name 'blanket' came from the fact that participants carried blankets for sleeping on the route because they were uncertain of accommodation, and most could not afford it anyway.

Neither of these marches ever reached London; the cavalry and local forces of law and order saw to that. Ringleaders were arrested and imprisoned, and the rest forced to return home before they had barely gone a few miles. There was a general sense of unrest in the country as anger and resentment built up over the injustices meted out to the working classes as the upper classes desperately tried to preserve the status quo. Charles Dickens, who was 7 at the time of Peterloo, later wrote that in July 1818,

> the Manchester Spinners, restless under their distress, had begun to realise the necessity of organization and of united action. Unable to resist the oppressions of greedy wealth, hunger had driven them to union. They met daily; they subscribed to support each other during strikes; they chose delegates. These meetings sometimes led to dangerous collisions.

Chapter 2

Female Reform Societies

It is time to effect a revolution in female manners – time to restore them to their lost dignity – and make them, as a part of the human species ...

A Vindication of the Rights of Woman,
Mary Wollstonecraft, 1792

Mary Wollstonecraft did not live to see Peterloo, but she did live to see the ugly sprawling tentacles of the Industrial Revolution spread over England's 'green and pleasant land'. Agricultural workers poured into the north-western towns and cities from the countryside, lured by the tales of more work, better conditions and higher pay than down on the farms. On twenty-first century social media sites this would be termed 'fake news', and so it turned out to be, but there was no going back. Thousands upon thousands found themselves trapped by poverty, deprivation and degradation in a noisy miserable smoke-filled hell that blocked out the sun for which the term 'dark Satanic mills' was too kind a description. A world of massive seven-storey mills, whose tall chimneys belched black clouds day and night, with the constant deafening noise of hundreds of fast-working mechanical looms and spinning frames (which rendered many workers totally deaf) for low wages, long hours, and a complete disregard for health and safety.

It was in 1817 that the involvement of radical females in politics first began to be noticed. A Manchester magistrate noted that,

the women of the lower class seem to take a strong part against the preservation of good order and in the course of the morning of the 10th, it was very general and undisguised cry amongst them that the gentry had had the upper hand long enough and that their turn has now come.

The following year, in 1818, Sam Bamford noted women's rights to attend political meetings.

At one of these meetings, which took place at Lydgate, in Saddleworth ... I, in the course of an address, insisted on the right, and the propriety also, of females who were present at such assemblages, voting by show of hand, for, or against the resolutions. This was a new idea; and the women, who attended numerously on that bleak ridge, were mightily pleased with it, – and the men being nothing dissentient, – when the resolution was put, the women held up their hands, amidst much laughter; and ever from that time females voted with the men at radical meetings. I was not then aware, that the new impulse thus given to political movement, would in a short time be applied to charitable and religious purposes. But it was so; our females voted at every subsequent meeting; it became the practice, – female political unions were formed, with their chair-women, committees, and other officials.

This was bad enough, but the burden on women was greater. After working twelve- or fourteen-hour shifts, men would expect to go home to a meal on the table and then down to the local pub to spend their hard-earned cash, and often that of their wives as well, on drinking themselves into oblivion. Women were expected to be utterly devoted to their husbands, to come home from a twelve-hour day in the mills to cook, clean and care for their children, and to put up and shut up about the problems of life. Once the wedding ring was on her finger, a woman lost her independence, her property, her basic civil rights, and even any control over her own body. For many, life was little better than that of a slave, and sometimes a great deal worse. As more than one Manchester cynic put it, marriage was simply a form of legalised prostitution crossed with slavery. A wife was required to allow her husband conjugal rights whenever he demanded them. Her feelings or physical comfort were simply not an issue. If she was ill, in pain, recovering from childbirth, or sore from beatings, it was irrelevant. She had no rights over her own body, which now belonged to her husband. She had no rights over her own possessions either, or any wages she earned. Literally everything she owned, even herself, became her husband's property on marriage. Coventry Patmore, a well-known Victorian poet, wrote 'The Angel in the House' in 1854, in which he declared that 'the perfect wife had to put her husband's happiness first in everything', and that 'she should worship him after death, sacrificing her own happiness to preserve his memory'. The 'angel in the house' had to be 'passive, self-sacrificing, meek, submissive, charming, pious, full of selfless devotion, sympathetic, devoid of any power of her own, and chastely pure'.

That, of course, was a ridiculous pipe-dream, especially in the appalling conditions of the millscapes, and women's reform associations, as well as those for men, had begun to be formed in the years before Peterloo. As Mary Wollstonecraft had written some twenty years before,

I then would fain convince reasonable men of the importance of some of my remarks; and prevail on them to weigh dispassionately the whole tenor of my observations. – I appeal to their understandings; and, as a fellow-creature, claim, in the name of my sex, some interest in their hearts. I entreat them to assist to emancipate their companion, to make her a help meet for them! Would men but generously snap our chains and be content with rational fellowship instead of slavish obedience, they would find us more observant daughters, more affectionate sisters, more faithful wives, more reasonable mothers – in a word, better citizens.

On 5 July 1819 a large open-air meeting was held in Blackburn demanding political reform. The *Manchester Observer* correctly surmised that those dubbed 'the swinish multitude' by the Tories were intending to take their fight for a fair democratic parliamentary system all the way to the heart of government. The paper wrote that, 'They now begin to see that the people have more weight than themselves, and if we mistake not, they will soon begin to feel the scale preponderate on the side of those, they have hitherto been treating with such insolence and contempt.'

Blackburn Female Reform Society

The Blackburn Female Reform Society was formed by a lady named Alice Kitchen on that same day, 5 July 1819, and they sent out circulars to other districts encouraging women from all classes to form similar associations promoting democratic ideals and objectives, and also actively encouraging participation by women in political matters:

> had it not been for the golden prize of reform held out to us, that weak and impotent as might be our strength, we should long ere thus have sallied forth to demand our rights, and in the acquirement of those rights to have obtained that food and raiment for our children, which God and nature have ordained for every living creature; but which our oppressors and tyrannical rulers have withheld from us.

The Blackburn Female Reformers were determined to make their mark. According to the *Leeds Mercury*, the women, 'dressed very neatly for the occasion', attended another outdoor public reform meeting in Blackburn to present the chairman, John Knight, with a special gift, 'a most beautiful Cap of Liberty, made of scarlet silk or satin. Lined with green, with a serpentine gold lace, terminating in a rich gold tassel ...' Afterwards, Alice Kitchen made a short speech and a plea to him.

Will you Sir, accept this token of our respect to these brave men who are nobly struggling for liberty and life: by placing it at the head of your banner, you will confer a lasting obligation on the Female Reformers of Blackburn. We shall esteem it as an additional favour, if the address which I deliver into your hands, be read to the Meeting: it embraces a faint description of our woes and may apologise for our interference in the politics of our country.

The banner was lowered and 'crowned by the Cap of Liberty'. A Cap of Liberty, also known as a Phrygian cap, is 'a soft conical cap with the apex bent over'. It became known as a Cap of Liberty when it was awarded to emancipated Roman slaves as a symbol of their freedom in a tribute to Libertas, the Roman god of freedom or liberty. In later centuries it became a symbol of the French Revolutionaries, representing the non-monarchical state, and was known as the French 'bonnet rouge'. A few years later it was adopted as a symbol of freedom by the oppressed and often starving workers of the English Industrial Revolution, particularly in the north of England.

After the presentation and amid great cheers from the crowd, the chairman read the address, which outlined the women's grievances, their wretched conditions, the plight of their hungry children, their pleas for a fair and democratic parliamentary system, and ending,

we the Female Reformers of Blackburn, therefore earnestly entreat you and every man in England, in the most solemn manner, to come forward and join the general union, that by a determined and constitutional resistance to our oppressors, the people may obtain annual parliaments, universal suffrage and election by ballot, which alone can save us from lingering misery and premature death. We look forward with horror to an approaching winter, when the necessity of food, clothing, and every requisite will increase double-fold

Black Dwarf, 14 July 1819

Afterwards a vote of thanks to the Female Reformers was carried by the crowd and presented to them by the chairman. The women had achieved a spectacular diplomatic coup. They were congratulated by the radical *Black Dwarf*, but condemned by the *Manchester Courier* for 'abandoning domestic considerations for political consideration'. The newspaper was scathing in its attack on the women:

of the degraded females who thus exhibited themselves, we know nothing, and should care less, if we did not discern, in their conduct the strongest proof of the corruption of their husbands, fathers and brothers. We consider, therefore, the fact of these women, thus deserting their station, as a painful evidence that their male kindred, in the pursuit of their guilty objects, have disunited themselves from those social ties and endearments which are the best pledges of their fidelity to their God, their country and their King ... we have lately witnessed a new contrivance for the ruin of society: Female Establishments, for demoralizing the rising generation: Mothers instructed to train their infants to the hatred of everything that is orderly and decent, and to rear up Rebels against God and State. Hitherto, this diabolical attempt has been confined to the most degraded of the sex: and it is to be hoped, that no woman who has a spark of virtue or honour remaining in her character, will engage in a scheme so disgusting and abominable.

The Blackburn women were also cruelly derided as lewd and licentious drunken harridans by George Cruickshank in his infamously misogynistic cartoon 'The Belle Alliance'; but they also had their supporters. William Cobbett was a farmer, soldier, writer, traveller and 'an archaic conservative'. He became a radical because of his contempt for corrupt government and he wanted to see an end to 'borough-mongers' (men who bought or sold parliamentary seats in English boroughs), 'rotten boroughs' and the Corn Laws. Cobbett was fulsome in his praise of the Blackburn female reformers as *Black Dwarf* reported.

> Never was there a paper that did more honour to its authors than did this address. Unaffected, clear, strong eloquent and pathetic; the heart that dictated it is worthy of the fairest and most tender bosom, and the heart that remains unarmed by it is unworthy of the breast of a human being. We shall, by and by, see this address, side by side with the address of a Queen; and then, we will challenge the 'higher orders' to a comparison of the two. The men, of what our foes have the insolence to call the 'lower orders' have, long since, shown their superiority, in point of mind, over the self-styled 'higher orders', and now we have before us the proof that our sisters surpass them in the same degree. We have too long, much too long, had the false modesty to admit, as a matter of course, that we were inferior to them in knowledge and talent. This gross and mischievous error is now, thank God, corrected.

Manchester Female Reform Society

The formation of the Blackburn Female Reform Society was followed on 20 July by the establishment of the Manchester Female Reform Society under the presidency of Mary Fildes, a well-known female radical. The new society put out an initial address to women of the middle and upper classes.

> Dear Sisters of the Earth, It is with a spirit of peaceful consideration and due respect that we are induced to address

you, upon the causes that have compelled us to associate together in aid of our suffering children, our dying parents, and the miserable partners of our woes. Bereft, not only of that support, the calls of nature require for existence; but the balm of sweet repose hath long been a stranger to us. Our minds are filled with a horror and despair, fearful on each returning morn, the light of heaven should present to us the corpse of some of our famished offspring, or nearest kindred, which the more kind hand of death had released from the oppressor.

Mary Fildes

Mary Fildes was born Mary Pritchard in 1789 near Cork on the west coast of Ireland. After coming to England, she met William Fildes, a Cheshire reed maker, and married him in the early spring of 1808. They had eight children: seven sons and one daughter. Mary, a passionate advocate of radical thought and action, named three of her sons after Thomas Paine (*Rights of Man*) and the noted radicals Henry Hunt and John Cartwright. She was involved in an early campaign for birth control, the idea of which was unthinkable at that time, and she was widely accused of distributing pornography.

Susannah Saxton

Susannah Saxton was the society's secretary. Her husband, John Saxton, a cotton worker and journalist, would stand on the hustings with Henry Hunt and would subsequently be imprisoned for this act. She wrote a number of pamphlets and public addresses. The members of Manchester Female Reform Society often put their case using Biblical references.

Noah was a reformer; he warned the people of their danger, but they paid no attention to him; Lot did in like manner, but the deluded people laughed him to scorn; the consequence was they were destroyed ... the great Founder of Christianity, he was the greatest reformer of all; and if Jesus Christ himself were to come upon the earth again ... his life would assuredly be sacrificed by the relentless hand of the Borough-Judases; for corruption, tyranny, and injustice, have reached their summit; and the bitter cup of oppression is now full to the brim.

Manchester Observer, 31 July 1819

Blackburn Female Reform Society were a little more prosaic about the situation.

> ... our houses which once bore ample testimony of our industry and cleanliness ... are now alas! robbed of all their ornaments ... by the relentless hand of the unfeeling tax gatherer, to satisfy ... the borough-mongering tyrants, who are reposing on beds of down.
>
> *Black Dwarf*, 14 July 1819

There were similar societies formed in Oldham, Royton and Stockport.

Stockport Female Reform Society

In their Articles of Association, women of the Stockport Society explained that it had basically been founded 'for the purpose of co-operating with their male associates' and continued:

> We who form and constitute the Stockport Female Union Society, having reviewed for a considerable time past the apathy, and frequent insult of our oppressed countrymen, by those sordid and all-devouring fiends, the Borough-mongering Aristocracy, and in order to accelerate the emancipation of this suffering nation, we, do declare, that we will assist the Male Union formed in this town, with all the might and energy that we possess, and that we will adhere to the principles, etc., of the Male Union ... and assist our Male friends to obtain legally, the long-lost Rights and Liberties of our country.

They went on, according to the *Lancaster Gazette* of 31 July 1819, to say that their aims were also to,

> collectively and individually to instil into the minds of our children a thorough knowledge of their natural and inalienable rights, whereby they shall be able to form just and correct notions of those legalised banditti of plunderers, who rob their parents of more than half the produce of their labours; we also pledge ourselves to stimulate our husbands, and sons to imitate the ancient Romans, who fought to a man in defence of their liberty and our daughters and female friends to imitate the Spanish women, who, when their husbands, sons and other kindred had gone out to fight in defence of their freedom, would rather have heard of the death of any of them, than their deserting the standard of liberty.

At a subsequent meeting on 19 July their president, Mrs Hallworth, put it rather more strongly.

> I am young, but Ladies, young as I am, I can assure you that the Borough villains have furnished me with such a woeful life of wretched experience, that I can feel for myself, and equally with myself, feel for my injured plundered country-women … we must unite and persevere until we fully possess those constitutional liberties and privileges which are the birth-right of every English man and woman.

She was supported by Miss Whalley who also addressed the meeting.

> Mrs President and Sisters, I love liberty and hate slavery. I know too truly the horrors of the one, and the virtues of the other. If a Borough-monger were to come to Stockport and be compelled to weave for his living, he would more impatiently (when he saw he could get nothing more than a mess of pottage

for his labour) cry out for Liberty and Reform! As well as those who are called the incorrigible swine, the disaffected, and the lower orders. I will not detain you, I have only to say that I could wish us to have a Cap of Liberty, and present it at the next Public Meeting, as our sisters at Blackburn did at theirs; and that we form the determination to bring it victoriously back again, or lose our lives in its defence.

Royton Female Reform Society

Royton women made both their political and personal feelings plain by the wording on the banner they carried at Peterloo. 'Annual Parliaments and Death to those in Authority who Oppose their Adoption. Let Us Die Like Men and Not Be Sold Like Slaves.' The message was unequivocal.

Black Dwarf welcomed these developments.

I have news to tell thee – news that will make thy heart leap with satisfaction; as I know thee to be an admirer of female heroism and a zealous advocate for the rights of women, as well as of the rights of man … Here the ladies are determined at last to speak for themselves; and they address their brother reformers in very manly language.

Harriet Martineau

Harriet was 17 years old when Peterloo took place. She was born into a Unitarian family and brought up in Norwich, where her father was a textile manufacturer (Norwich and East Anglia were renowned for their woollen goods); unusually, she grew up in a family where all the children, both girls and boys, were encouraged to read widely. Harriet did not attend Peterloo, although she would have known about it and read about it. She made her living as a writer on sociological, domestic and feminine issues and she said of her work that 'when one studies a society, one must focus on all its aspects, including key political, religious and social institutions.' She had close links with Charles Darwin's family and strong views on female education.

> The intellect of women is confined by an unjustifiable restriction of ... education ... As women have none of the objects in life for which an enlarged education is considered requisite, the education is not given ... The choice is to either be ill-educated, passive, and subservient, or well-educated, vigorous, and free only upon sufferance.

History has judged Harriet Martineau as the first real sociologist, but to the Victorians she was controversial because she criticised slavery and the lack of female education, and supported women's suffrage, the Married Woman's Property Act, and the licensing of prostitution. Nevertheless, she won the favour of the young Queen Victoria and was invited to her wedding.

Mary Shelley

Mary Shelley was 22 years old at the time of Peterloo. She was born in London, the daughter of political philosopher, William Godwin, and writer Mary Wollstonecraft. Her mother died when she was about a month old and she was brought up by her father, who gave her a wide-ranging education. When she was 15 her father described her as 'singularly bold, somewhat imperious, and active of mind. Her desire of knowledge is great, and her perseverance in everything she undertakes almost invincible.' She married the poet Percy Bysshe Shelley, who wrote the 'Masque of Anarchy', a grieving commemoration of Peterloo, although both of them were in Italy when Peterloo took place. Her most famous novel, *Frankenstein*, was written as a ghost story during the cold wet 'summer that never was' of 1816 at Lord Byron's house in Geneva; but Mary continued writing and editing throughout her life and, like her mother, she also strongly supported the causes of women.

Jessie Potter

Jessie was 18 years old when Peterloo took place. A local beauty, she was born and raised in Lancaster, the daughter of Abraham Crompton, a member of Lancaster's mayoral family. She married Edmund Potter, who was a millowner in Glossop, Derbyshire, and whose family owned land and textile warehouses in central Manchester. Edmund Potter, like Jessie, was a Unitarian and full of radical ideas which Jessie quickly adopted as her own, becoming known as 'the pretty radical'. He was also a benevolent millowner, caring about his employees, providing cheap food from local farms, organising basic part-time schooling for their children and building a library within his extensive mill complex for the use of his workers. Their second son, Rupert, was the father of children's author, Beatrix Potter, who was heavily influenced by Jessie's views.

Attitudes towards radical women

The reaction from the more conservative newspapers, however, was predictable. The *Manchester Chronicle* (founded by Charles Wheeler in 1781) condemned the Blackburn Female Reformers and their actions in presenting a Cap of Liberty and asking for their pleas to be read aloud as 'disgusting', and justified its conclusion with the statement that 'these women then mixed with the orators and remained on the hustings for the rest of the day. The public scarcely need to be informed, that the females are known to be the most abandoned of their sex'. Cartoonists depicted them as 'lewd and crude', smoking, drinking, and displaying all parts of their bodies in inappropriate ways. The Stockport Sunday School followed suit with an almost hysterical denouncement of radical women, repeating the *Manchester Courier*'s condemnation that,

> we have lately witnessed a new contrivance for the ruin of society: Female Establishments for demoralizing the rising generation; Mothers instructed to train their infants to the

hatred of everything that is orderly and decent, and to rear up rebels against God and the State. Hitherto, this diabolical attempt has been confined to the most degraded of the sex ...

The *Manchester Chronicle* weighed in again with an assertion that female reformers 'presented a spectacle very revolting to those notions of female delicacy which are so natural to Englishmen'. The hypocrisy was astonishing and must have greatly offended contemporary women like Harriet Martineau, Mary Shelley, and Jessie Potter.

Although nineteenth-century women involved in politics and radical thought were cruelly demeaned and brutally dismissed by the all-male establishment, they were much more tolerated by working-class men because working-class men were suffering badly as well. Many working-class women had the foresight to see that if they offered support to their men, helping to win them concessions, increased pay and, more importantly, the vote, then they would benefit as well. Few men thought quite that far ahead. Their wives and families were working hard to support them and in their eyes that was perfectly acceptable. The bitterest irony, however, was that middle-class and upper-class members of female reform societies did not want working-class women involved. Like their sisters in the suffragette movements over half a century later, they believed that the material poverty of the working classes meant that working-class people were lesser persons of lower intelligence. This was simply not true, but the class system in Britain had been entrenched for centuries, although since the early eighteenth century, for material reasons rather than those of birth and rank. Today (2020) the class system is still strong in Britain, far more so than in most other Western countries. Financial wealth still determines social status, personal worth, educational resources and employment opportunities, and the belief remains, even in the twenty-first century, that working-class people are lesser persons of lower intelligence despite a wealth of evidence to the contrary.

Chapter 3

Prologue to Peterloo

Monday, 16 August 1819 dawned a dry, warm sunny day, typical of the harvest season. In the suburbs and townships of Manchester, families prepared themselves for a day out and the excitement of hearing the distinguished orator, Henry Hunt, suggest how they could improve their lot by campaigning for a fair democratic system, representation in Parliament and universal franchise (for men anyway). Monday was traditionally the weavers' day off, and many of those who intended going were weavers. The weaving industry was depressed, and wages were very low. This, coupled with the introduction of the Corn Laws after the Napoleonic Wars which was keeping the price of bread high, encouraged those attending the meeting to add the demand of a fair day's pay for a fair day's work to their pleas for democracy and the franchise.

The working classes had little enough, but most had a 'Sunday best' outfit which, although it might be shabby, would be scrupulously clean and mended. The fashion then was for 'Empire line' dresses which had no waist, but were gathered under the bustline, and then fell directly to the feet. They were not made for running. Most of the contingents marched in neat columns of five across, and this gave rise to some unease among those watching who felt that there might be a military aspect involved. It was known that there had been drilling sessions in some of the townships and Mary Collins from Failsworth said that she attended dawn drilling sessions up on nearby White Moss. This had been instigated by march leaders like Samuel Bamford who led the Middleton contingent; it was felt that a neat orderly march would present a more businesslike front than a higgledy-piggledy collection of stragglers. Some of the men had whispered about carrying sticks, but this had been expressly forbidden by orator Hunt who was insisting on a completely peaceful march and meeting. He wrote a letter a few days before Peterloo.

> You will meet on Monday next, my friends, and by your *steady, firm and temperate* deportment, you will convince all your enemies, that you feel you have an *important*, and an *imperious public duty* to perform; and that you will not suffer any private consideration on earth to deter you from exerting every nerve to carry your praiseworthy and patriotic intentions. The eyes of all England, nay, of all Europe, are fixed upon you; and every friend of real Reform, and of rational Liberty, is tremblingly alive to the results of your Meeting on Monday next. OUR ENEMIES will seek every opportunity, by the means of their sanguinary agents, to excite a RIOT, that they may have a pretence for SPILLING OUR BLOOD, reckless of the awful and certain retaliation that would ultimately fall on their heads …. Come, then, my friends to the Meeting on Monday, *armed* with NO OTHER WEAPON but that of a self-approving conscience; determined not to suffer youselves to be irritated or excited, by any means whatsoever, to commit any breaches of the public peace.

Samuel Bamford records in his memoirs that,

> Twelve of the most decent-looking youths … were placed at the front, each with a branch of laurel held in his hand, as a token of peace; then the colours [banners]: a blue one of silk, with inscriptions in golden letters, 'Unity and Strength', 'Liberty and Fraternity'; a green one of silk, with golden letters, 'Parliaments Annual', 'Suffrage Universal'. They marched smartly along the road and Bamford continued 'on the bank of an open field on our left I perceived a gentleman observing us attentively. He beckoned me, and I went to him. He was one of

my late employers. He took my hand, and rather concernedly, but kindly, said he hoped no harm was intended by all those people who were coming in. I said 'I would pledge my life for their entire peaceableness.' I asked him to notice them, 'did they look like persons wishing to outrage the law? were they not, on the contrary, evidently heads of decent working families? or members of such families?' 'No, no,' I said, 'my dear sir, and old respected master, if any wrong or violence take place, they will be committed by men of a different stamp from these.' He said he was very glad to hear me say so; he was happy he had seen me and gratified by the manner in which I had expressed myself. I asked, did he think we should be interrupted at the meeting? he said he did not believe we should; 'then,' I replied, 'all will be well'; and shaking hands, with mutual good wishes, I left him, and took my station as before.

It is difficult to visualise the empty space of St Peter's Field today. It took its name from St Peter's Church which stood on the site of the present tram stop complex. The Town Hall, Central Library, the Midland Hotel, Manchester Central, the Theatre Royal and the Free Trade Hall (now Radisson Blu Hotel) did not exist. The ground on which they now stand was all open field. The magistrates had assembled at 11 am to watch the proceedings in Mr Cooper's cottage, which stood approximately on the site of the present Mr Cooper's Restaurant in the Midland Hotel. The hustings were a little further down on the corner of South Street with Windmill Street, to which the magistrates had a direct line of sight. At around midday, special constables lined the path to the hustings which orator Henry Hunt's carriage would take. Cheshire Yeomanry were then lined up along Windmill Street and the Manchester Yeomanry were stationed on Cooper Street, which at that time extended past the present Central Library to a junction with Mount Street, while the Hussars were positioned close to the magistrates. The stage was now set for the tragedy which would ensue.

Chapter 4

Peterloo

J oseph Nadin, the deputy chief constable of Manchester, was a ruthless man; totally unsympathetic to the plight of workers and determined to keep law and order at any cost, he employed spies to attend Hampden Club meetings. Based on their reports, Nadin arrested a large number of men for 'political offences and attending seditious meetings'. In March 1819, the Hampden Clubs in the Manchester area had amalgamated and became the Patriotic Union Society. Joseph Johnson was secretary and James Wroe (of the radical *Manchester Observer*) was treasurer. The society decided to hold a mass meeting in Manchester on the subject of electoral reform to be addressed by Henry Hunt, and by Richard Carlile, a keen exponent of universal suffrage and freedom of the press who had been greatly influenced by Thomas Paine's book *The Rights of Man*. John Cartwright was also invited, but was unable to attend. The meeting to be held on St Peter's Fields was eventually allowed to go ahead on 16 August 1819, after much wrangling with local magistrates, but it was barely thirty years since the French Revolution and the authorities were nervous. It had, therefore, been decided that troops, including the Manchester Yeomanry and Cheshire Hussars, should stand by at St Peter's Field in case of civil disorder.

The Peterloo meeting on Monday, 16 August 1819 should have been a peaceful, sober meeting on a warm summer's day. Many men wore white shirts and some carried bunches of laurel, while a sizeable number of women wore white dresses to symbolise purity, and greenery in their hair to symbolise friendship and peace. Although not born until 1825, the noted Failsworth author Ben Brierley later wrote about the role of women in the march to Peterloo,

> the procession marched to St Peter's Field, led by the beautiful and heroic Jane Winterbottom and her fair sisterhood, each clad in a vesture of white with bays woven in their hair, and carrying imitations of the olive branch in their hands, as emblems of a peaceful purpose, the black flag bearing the motto 'liberty or death' floated behind them.

Samuel Bamford who was leading the marchers from Middleton wrote:

> Our whole column, with the Rochdale people, would probably consist of six thousand men. At our head were a hundred or two of women, mostly young wives, and mine own was amongst them. A hundred or two of our handsomest girls, – sweethearts to the lads who were with us – danced to the music, or sung snatches of popular songs: a score or two of children were sent back, though some went forward; whilst, on each side of our line walked some thousands of stragglers. And this, accompanied by our friends, and our nearest and most tender connections, we went slowly towards Manchester.

Francis Philips had watched the procession from Stockport:

> On the 16th August I went on the Stockport Road about eleven or a little after, and I met a great number of persons advancing towards Manchester with all the regularity of a regiment, only they had no uniform. They were all marching in file, principally three abreast. They had two banners with them. There were persons by the side, acting as officers and regulating the files. The order was beautiful indeed.

Another observer of Peterloo wrote:

> The Reformers, who seemed determined to make this a splendid
> day … in preparing flags and small bands of music, and in
> arranging matters for the approaching meeting. It is evident,
> however, from the great number of females, and even children,
> who formed part of the procession, that nothing was anticipated
> that could involve them in the least degree of peril; and an
> immense multitude gathered together, relying in confidence on
> each other's peaceful intentions, and certainly not expecting,
> that the precautions taken by the magistracy to preserve the
> peace, would be employed to destroy it, and convert a peaceable
> assembly into a scene of terror and alarm, danger and death.

The women were also responsible for making the colourful banners
proclaiming REFORM, UNIVERSAL SUFFRAGE, EQUAL
REPRESENTATION, and even LOVE. They also made the red silk
caps denoting liberty, which topped many of the poles. The mottoes
were strikingly similar to the cry of 'LIBERTÉ, EQUALITÉ,
FRATERNITÉ' which had characterised the French Revolution just
thirty years before Peterloo. The aim was to make a strong visual impact
while emphasising their peaceful conduct. Folk filed excitedly into St
Peter's Field, or Place as it was sometimes known, and waited for Henry
Hunt to arrive. However, the government and the elite, entitled, and
wealthy aristocracy had reacted with anger and alarm to what they saw
as these radical groups actually demanding to be given some rights,
because to agree to their demands would weaken their control over
what they believed should be a grateful and submissive population.

A couple of days before the meeting members of the Manchester
Yeomanry had been ordered to have their sabres newly sharpened. By
lunchtime on 16 August the crowd had swelled to between 60,000–80,000
people (exact numbers are virtually impossible to assess; some even
suggested as many as 150,000–300,000 attended) although, according

to contemporary eye-witness accounts, the mood was peaceful and good natured. When Henry Hunt arrived at the hustings with his colleagues Samuel Bamford, John Saxton, and Mary Fildes, there was a roar of welcome and applause. Watching the proceedings from Cooper's Cottage were nine magistrates, including: William Hulton (who appeared to be the chief magistrate), J. Norris, John Entwisle, J. Home, W. Marriott, Thos. Wm Tatton, R. Marsh, Trafford Trafford and Ralph Fletcher. They were already very nervous about the situation, but seeing the response of the crowd to the arrival of Henry Hunt, they now panicked. At this point the Riot Act should have been read and the crowd allowed to disperse peacefully, but contemporary eye-witness accounts, including that of a bishop who had called on the magistrates and was watching proceedings from an upper window, said that had not happened. Instead, desperate to keep control, the magistrates ordered the Manchester Yeomanry to break up the meeting and arrest Henry Hunt. During the morning, the Yeomanry had been plied with ale and by lunchtime most of them were in various stages of drunkenness. When the order came to arrest Hunt all they could see was a field tightly packed with people. In their befuddled minds there was only one way to clear a path through and when someone shouted 'Charge!' they drew their sabres, kicked their horses into action and thundered down what is now Cooper Street. The first casualty of the day occurred as on the way they knocked a 2-year-old child, William Fildes (the son of Ann and Charles Fildes who lived in Kennedy Street), from his mother's arms as she tried to get out of their way. Ann Fildes watched in horror and disbelief as their horses trampled the toddler to death. The Yeomanry rode on without stopping and, on reaching St Peter's Field, they slashed right and left with their sabres to clear a path through the crowd, ignoring the screams of pain and fear from men, women and children felled by sabres and then trampled by the horses as they fled in terror. In the words of Samuel Bamford:

> On the cavalry drawing up they were received with a shout of goodwill, as I understood it. They shouted again, waving their

sabres over their heads; and then, slackening rein, and striking spur into their steeds, they dashed forward and began cutting the people. 'Stand fast,' I said, 'they are riding upon us; stand fast.' The cavalry were in confusion: they evidently could not, with all the weight of man and horse, penetrate that compact mass of human beings and their sabres were plied to hew a way through naked held-up hands and defenceless heads; and then chopped limbs and wound-gaping skulls were seen; and groans and cries were mingled with the din of that horrid confusion.

Many females appeared as the crowd opened; and striplings or mere youths also were found. Their cries were piteous and heart-rending, and would, one might have supposed, have disarmed any human resentment: but here their appeals were in vain. In ten minutes from the commencement of the havoc the field was an open and almost deserted space. The sun looked down through a sultry and motionless air. The curtains and blinds of the windows within view were all closed.

The day before the meeting, St Peter's Field had been cleared of sticks, stones, or anything that might be used as a weapon of either attack or defence. Mary Collins believed that this had been done because the cavalry attack was premeditated. Desperately trying to escape, a small group of people knocked one member of the Yeomanry from his horse. On seeing this, one of the magistrates turned to the detachment of Hussars and Dragoons and yelled 'Good God! Can't you see they're attacking the Yeomanry!' This was the signal for even more military personnel to enter the field. They, at least, appeared to be sober, and they showed more restraint than the Yeomanry as they rode to their assistance. However, those who were fleeing could not know this, so chaos and pandemonium increased. Within 10–15 minutes, despite the Yeomanry blocking some of the exits, St Peter's Field had emptied of those who could still walk or run.

Left behind was a bloody sprawl of dead and badly injured bodies lying on the ground. Hunt and his colleagues, Samuel Bamford, John Saxton, Joseph Healey and Joseph Johnson, were under arrest. Twenty people were dead or dying and 700 were injured, many badly. Thousands of survivors managed to drag themselves home and would go on to suffer what today is called Post Traumatic Stress Disorder (PTSD). The magistrates congratulated themselves on a good day's work and for keeping the peace. Eyewitnesses and journalists who had not been involved in the scrum were completely shocked by what they had witnessed. Joseph Barrett, from Newton Heath, said that the Yeomanry had seemed nervous at first but after the massacre they

> … went completely mad; they made about the streets of Manchester striking at every person that was in their way, and even went to one cotton mill and wished to strike the people that were coming out, and hacked at the doors'. He continued 'the morning after an ultra Tory came into our warehouse … and my brother said 'you made sad work with the people yesterday', and he replied 'we could do it better … by stopping up the ends of the streets … and planting cannon and killing every devil of them.'

Journalist James Wroe, the editor of the radical *Manchester Observer*, was responsible for naming the tragedy 'Peterloo' after the recently fought Battle of Waterloo in 1815. John Lees, from Oldham, who subsequently died of injuries received at Peterloo, had actually fought at Waterloo. He said that while it was fair fighting hand-to-hand at Waterloo, Peterloo was 'just downright murder'. The cavalry seemed to have directed their attacks more at the women, seeing this course of action as justified based on what they had heard and read about female reformers. A far higher percentage of injuries and deaths were recorded for the women who took part in Peterloo than for the men. Four of the eighteen deaths recorded were female, but there were more than were officially listed. The main thing that had seemed to enrage the cavalry, apart from females daring to attend and take part in a public meeting, were the flags with slogans advocating a fair democracy and a fair day's pay for a fair day's work and the 'Caps of Liberty', a symbol of the French Revolution which had happened only thirty years before Peterloo. Several women carried banners topped by Caps of Liberty and so they became prime objects for destruction.

Mary Fildes, the president of the Manchester Female Reform Society who had been invited to ride in Henry Hunt's carriage, had held such a banner aloft on the hustings; it read: 'Manchester Female Reform Society' on one side and 'Let us die like men and not be sold like slaves' on the reverse. She avoided the sabres until the hustings were surrounded when, for her own safety, she tried to leap down to the ground and escape. Her petticoats caught on a nail of the hustings and she hung briefly suspended in mid-air, and, as an eyewitness described it, she was 'slashed across her exposed body by one of the brave cavalry'. Although she was truncheoned across the head and sabred across her face, legs and breasts, she was not seriously wounded and escaped with some deep cuts and bruises. Mary immediately went into hiding to escape arrest lest her injuries should be seen and incriminate her.

Elizabeth Gaunt, Mary's terrified friend, was several months pregnant and tried to protect herself by hiding in Hunt's carriage. She was dragged out, hit, arrested and accused of treason. Gaunt's appearance lived up to her name. She was 'a tall thin pale woman in her mid-forties'. Thrown unceremoniously into a prison cell, her dress removed to wash out what might, for the authorities, be incriminating bloodstains from her injuries, she was left for thirty-six hours without food or water. She continued to be held in solitary confinement and was refused not only the food and clothing brought by her husband, but also any medical aid from doctors. For ten days she was 'dragged many times a day up a flight of stairs to be exhibited and questioned', until she was too weak to walk. She fainted during the hearings she faced with Hunt and the others. The *Observer* for 30 August 1819 reported that,

> the prisoner [Elizabeth Gaunt] came, or rather was carried from behind the dock where she had a seat ... she looked pale, emaciated and almost fainting for weakness in consequence of the [untended] wounds which she had received at the meeting and her subsequent solitary confinement.

On the twelfth day of her captivity she was finally released without charge. However, her ill treatment finally caused her to miscarry and she lost her baby. Despite her dreadful sufferings, she was one of the luckier ones in that she survived the experience at all.

Sarah Hargreaves, a leader of the Manchester Female Union and dressed all in black on the day, was also arrested, remanded and tried with Elizabeth Gaunt; she too was released after twelve days.

Mary Heys, who lived off Oxford Road, was less fortunate. She was,

> knocked down and trampled on by a cavalry horse, her foot stripped of the flesh and great toenails ... she was pregnant at the time and so much bruised ... she continued to have fits almost daily til ... she died ... prematurely delivered of a seven months child which caused her death.

Martha Partington from Eccles tried to flee but was caught, thrown into a cellar by the military which killed her outright, leaving two young children motherless.

Margaret Downes was badly slashed in the breast and was hidden away by her friends for fear of her suffering further injury and indignities. She was not heard of again and was presumed dead. It is most likely that she bled out from the wounds she had received.

Bridget Hagan of Lees Street was 'thrown down and rode over by the cavalry, thighs and body much hurt ... stomach hurt ... had a miscarriage in consequence'. She survived but was disabled as a result of her injuries.

Elizabeth Mellor of Ancoats, also pregnant, was thrown down and seriously hurt; it is not recorded if her baby survived.

Mary Orme, who lived off Deansgate, was an elderly lady of some 70 years in age. She was thrown to the ground and trampled on, which resulted in her hip being dislocated and her left leg being injured, leaving her permanently disabled.

Bridget Monks, another 70-year-old woman, who lived on Portland Street, had her right shoulder dislocated, received a sabre cut on her left arm, and her legs were hurt.

Elizabeth Neil/Neale, who lived on Queen Street, was trampled by the cavalry leaving her with broken arms, legs and ribs. She remained in hospital for a week and was forced to convalesce for at least a further seven weeks.

Sarah Jones, a mother of seven children who lived on Silk Street, was so badly beaten about the head with a constable's truncheon that she remained disabled for a long time. According to Henry Hunt, however, she was actually killed on the day.

One of the most detailed and disturbing descriptions of Peterloo comes from Jemima Bamford. She was the wife of Samuel Bamford who was on the hustings with Henry Hunt and also wrote at length on Peterloo. Jemima had badgered and bullied her husband to let her attend the meeting at St Peter's Field, but later confessed that she would have gone anyway, with or without his permission. Subsequently, shocked and dazed, Jemima wrote of Peterloo:

> I was determined to go to the meeting, and should have followed, even if my husband had refused his consent to my going with the procession. From what I, in common with others, had heard the week previous, 'that if the country people went with their caps of liberty, and their banners, and music, the soldiers would be brought to them,' I was uneasy,

and felt persuaded, in my own mind, that something would be the matter, and I had best go with my husband, and be near him; and if I only saw him I should be more content than in staying at home. I accordingly, he having consented after much persuasion, gave my little girl something to please her, and promising more on my return, I left her with a careful neighbour woman, and joined some other married females at the head of the procession. Every time I went aside to look at my husband, and that was often, an ominous impression smote my heart. He looked very serious, I thought, and I felt a foreboding of something evil to befall us that day.

I was dressed plainly as a countrywoman in my second-best attire. My companions were also neatly dressed as the wives of working men; I had seen Mr Hunt before that time; they had not, and some of them were quite eager to obtain good places, that they might see and hear one of whom so much had been reported.

In going down Mosley Street, I lost sight of my husband. Mrs Yates, who had hold of my arm, would keep hurrying forward to get a good place, and when the crowd opened for the Middleton procession, Mrs Yates and myself, and some others of the women, went close to the hustings, quite glad that we had obtained such a situation for seeing and hearing all. My husband got on the stage, but when afterwards I saw him leap down, and lost sight of him, I began to be unhappy. The crowd seemed to have increased very much, for we became insufferably pressed. We were surrounded by men who were strangers; we were almost suffocated, and to me the heat was quite sickening; but Mrs. Yates, being taller than myself, supported it better. I felt I could not bear this long, and I became alarmed. I reflected that if there was any more pressure, I must faint, and then what would become of me? I begged of the men to open a way and let me go out, but they would not move. Every moment I became worse, and I told some other men, who stood in a row, that I was sick, and begged they would let me pass them, and they immediately made a way, and I went down a long passage betwixt two ranks of these men, many of them saying, 'make way, she's sick, she's sick, let her go out,' and I passed quite out of the crowd and, turning to my right, I got on some high ground, on which stood a row of houses – this was Windmill Street.

I thought if I could get to stand at the door of one of those houses, I should have a good view of the meeting, and should perhaps see my husband again; and I kept going further down the row, until I saw a door open, and I stepped within it, the people of the house making no objections. By this time Mr Hunt was on the hustings, addressing the people. In a minute or two some soldiers came riding up. The good folks of the house, and some who seemed to be visitors, said, 'the soldiers were only come to keep order; they would not meddle with the people;' but I was alarmed. The people shouted, and then the soldiers shouted, waving their swords. Then they rode amongst the people, and there was a great outcry, and a moment after, a man passed without hat, and wiping the blood of his head with his hand, and it ran down his arm in a great stream.

The meeting was all in a tumult; there were dreadful cries; the soldiers kept riding amongst the people, and striking with their swords. I became faint, and turning from the door, I went unobserved down some steps into a cellared passage; and hoping to escape from the horrid noise, and to be concealed, I crept into a vault, and sat down, faint and terrified, on some fire wood. The cries of the multitude outside, still continued, and the people of the house, upstairs, kept bewailing most pitifully. They could see all the dreadful work through the window, and their exclamations were so distressing, that I put my fingers in my ears to prevent my hearing more; and on removing them, I understood that a young man had just been brought past, wounded. The front door of the passage before mentioned, soon after opened, and a number of men entered, carrying the body of a decent, middle aged woman, who had been killed. I thought they were going to put her beside me, and was about to scream, but they took her forward, and deposited her in some premises at the back of the house.

A Sarah Taylor, who lived on Mather Street, was cut on the head and bruised. She 'had hidden under the hustings and saw a man named John Ashton, who had carried the Saddleworth flag, sabred and trampled. He died two days later.' Ann Scott of Liverpool Road, was arrested on the evening of Peterloo and said she was 'violently laid of in Deansgate' and then taken to the New Bailey prison where she was held from Monday to Friday. She was allowed no bed and no toilet facilities and, as a result, became seriously ill. Later she made a statement in which she said:

Afterwards, when I had been a fortnight in the hospital, and suffering under a relapse of the fever, I was permitted to see my husband, for the first time since my arrest, although I had repeatedly entreated that he might be let in to speak to me; and when I saw him I was scarcely able to speak to him. He remained with me about ten minutes, when Jackson ordered him away ... About a fortnight afterwards, I was again allowed to see my husband: but he was not permitted to remain with me above ten minutes, the turnkey standing beside us during our conversation.

Ruth and Eddie Frow, *Political Women*

Martha Kearsley from Oldham had been close to the hustings. She said that panic was caused by 'the soldiers coming and cutting and slashing among the people.' She had seen 'a man fighting off two soldiers who were attacking him with swords when a third came up and wounded him on the back of the shoulder. I was so struck with horror, that I turned round and saw no more of him.' She also saw many others 'cut by the soldiers'.

Elizabeth Farren of Lombard Street, Manchester, said she had been cut on her forehead which was not completely healed. She said she was attacked as the cavalry went to the hustings. 'I was with my child and I was frightened for its safety, and to protect it, held it close to my side with head downwards, to avoid the blow. I desired them to spare my child, and I was directly cut on my forehead.' She lost consciousness and when she came round three hours later, she found herself in a cellar.

Hannah Croft lived on Windmill Street, which bounded St Peter's Fields. She looked out of the window and saw the Manchester cavalry riding among the crowd 'and the people falling in heaps … the people tried to get away but the soldiers rode so hard that they knocked them down before they could get out of the way.' Ann Jones also lived on Windmill Street; she told how she,

> … saw the cavalry cutting and slashing and saw a large quantity of blood on the field after they were gone … I saw a great many people wounded, and very bloody indeed … there was a great many people in my house, and all was in great confusion, and some of the special constables came up in great triumph before my door, calling out, 'This is Waterloo for you! This is Waterloo!'

Margaret Goodwin from Salford was between Saint Peter's church and the hustings. She saw 'two men wounded near the church all covered with blood and gore … and a woman cut within a few yards of where she was standing.' She was trying to get away when she was 'wounded by Thomas Shelmerdine and knocked unconscious'.

Ethelinda Wilson wrote articles in *Republican*, a journal published by the political and radical Richard Carlile. She 'condemned the failure of the male reformers to hold another meeting on St Peter's fields' and said 'it is now up to women to take up the fight. Future generations would thank them for doing so ... our mothers, our revered mothers, cultivated the soil in which this universal blessing grew.' When Ethelinda left Manchester for London, she attended meetings there touting a loaded pistol wrapped in a handkerchief.

Chapter 5

Post Peterloo

Afterwards, the protests began. Initially the authorities tried to dismiss the episode and pretend it had never happened, despite the appalling carnage, but there were too many witnesses and too much evidence. Appeals for justice were made to the highest in the land, but to little avail. The Prince Regent, far from being concerned, was cold and dismissive of the Peterloo massacre, choosing instead to praise and congratulate the magistrates and the military for their efficient and appropriate actions. Parliament followed suit. Lord Sidmouth, the home secretary, who had been responsible for the 'Gagging Acts', was particularly effusive in his praise of the magistrates and the Yeomanry. Returning on 23 November after recess, Lord Sidmouth decided that prompt action was needed over what John Scott, the lord chancellor, described as 'an overt act of treason', and advised the prime minister, Lord Liverpool, accordingly.

Robert Jenkinson, 2nd Earl of Liverpool, who became Lord Liverpool on the death of his father, was born in London, and received a public school and Oxford University education. A typical Conservative, favouring the interests of manufacturing and the landed gentry, he was prime minister from 1812 to 1827, and presided over the introduction of the Corn Laws in 1815 and higher taxation to help pay for the Napoleonic Wars. He had also had to deal with Luddite disturbances between 1811 and 1816, when Luddites (named after their leader, Ned Ludd) took action in destroying industrial textile machinery which they believed was robbing them of employment. Lord Liverpool had absolutely no idea and even less understanding of what life was actually like for the 'lower orders'. After Peterloo he sided with the Prince Regent and other members of government in congratulating the magistrates and the cavalry for their actions at Peterloo. Consequently, the result was the passing of what came to be known as the 'Six Acts'. 1) Training Prevention Act which made anyone attending training or drilling exercises (unless under military orders) liable to arrest and transportation for seven years. 2) Seizure of Arms Act giving local magistrates the power to search any person or property for arms. 3) Seditious Meetings Prevention Act. This prohibited public meetings of more than fifty people without the explicit consent of local magistrates. 4) Misdemeanours Act, which was supposed to reduce delay in justice being administered. 5) Blasphemous and Seditious Libels Act providing harsh punishments and/or banishment for any publications deemed to be of a blasphemous or seditious nature. 6) Newspaper and Stamp Duties Act, which ordered radical publications to pay the stamp duty that they had previously avoided by publishing opinions rather than news.

These Acts were staunchly opposed by the Whigs (Liberals), and one angry reformer wrote of the parliamentarians who had backed these measures 'I despair of being able adequately to express correct ideas of the singular baseness, the detestable infamy, of their equally mean and murderous conduct.'

The Six Acts were designed to stifle any further protest by the 'lower orders'. Although the Acts were mostly repealed by the mid-nineteenth century, the Training Prevention Act was not repealed until 2008. Habeas Corpus was also suspended for a short period as it had been with the Gagging Acts prior to Peterloo. This new set of repressive Acts were badly received, coming so soon after the Gagging Acts. There were many protests, and a witty Northern poet calling himself Geoffrey Gag-'em-all, wrote a sixteen-page poem expressing horror and indignation at this further infringement of civil liberties. It began,

John Bull through twenty years of war
To liberty had some pretences

But six years of peace and six new acts
Have reft him of his seven senses.

His sense of smelling is fast closed
His mouth is by a padlock bound
His ears are plugged where sound reposed
His fingers cutting thumbscrews wound.

All that the appetite can court
Is placed within his aching view
He cannot touch, or smell, or taste,
Forbidden by the Six Acts New.

(Oldham Historical Research Association)

The *Manchester Observer* was closed down because of its radical views and because of James Wroe coining the name Peterloo for the massacre that had taken place. In the weeks after the massacre, the authorities also targeted female relatives of reformers, as detailed by Joseph Johnson in a letter published in the *Black Dwarf* on 29 September.

Not content with multiplying indictments upon Mr Wroe, the intrepid proprietor of the Manchester Observer, and exasperated at his perseverance, and their incapacity to obtain possession of his person, the revengeful animals have directed all the engines of their prostituted authority to the persecution of his wife and children, who continue to sell that and other obnoxious publications. Twice have the mean violators of the law and deciders of justice held Mrs Wroe to bail, and twice have her children been taken out of his shop, and sureties been demanded for their appearance to answer the charge of having published scandalous libels, that told too much truth of these Manchester magistrates ... In addition to Mrs Wroe, the wife of one of the journeymen, Mrs Hough and her daughter, were arrested and confined in the New Bailey all night.

William Cobbett had taken up the Reformers' cause and he defended them staunchly. His efforts did not go unappreciated and the female reformers of Manchester issued a grateful address to him in late November.

> It cannot be unknown to you, Sir, that our intentions have been vilified, and our characters traduced by the unprincipled scribes, of a venal and corrupt press. To you, in your excellent letter to the Female Reformers of Blackburn, we are indebted for a complete vindication of our motives, our conduct and our characters; you have refuted the calumnies of our enemies and proved our innocence and integrity. The days of chivalry are passed; but in you the Female Reformers feel that they shall never want a sufficient advocate.

Four months after Peterloo, a general meeting planned by Warrington inhabitants was compulsorily cancelled after an address to the Prince Regent, 'by clergy, gentry, merchants, manufacturers and other inhabitants' of the town who were 'defending the laws and constitution of these realms' and who,

> deeply deplore that the liberty of the press has so fearfully degenerated into licentiousness, and become the medium of propagation of opinions replete with infidelity and treason … and we view with abhorrence the conduct of rebellious emissaries, who, by their inflammatory and seditious harangues, endeavor to seduce unthinking men from their religion and allegiance; and who, by garbled representations and willful misconstructions of the late occurrences of this immediate neighbourhood, attempt to keep alive the spirit

of insubordination which, unfortunately, they have been too successful in inviting.

In short, the working classes should know their place, then shut up and put up. There was a great fear of 'the designs and practices of the disaffected which ... would entirely put a stop to trade, manufactures and labour.' Despite the antiquated language, most of these sentiments can still be recognised today. Capitalism and profits rely on labour. Raw materials and manufacturing processes are difficult to reduce, but labour costs are much easier to cut. Although slavery has long been officially abolished, there is still talk of employing 'slave labour', because low labour costs mean increased profits. However, for working people, their labour is often all they have to sell and they need a fair return. Everyone is entitled to make a decent living. The option of withdrawing labour is a powerful tool because, without labour, commercial success and profits will suffer. Therefore, the strict control of workers was seen as essential for continuing profits. It is a difficult conundrum which still awaits a satisfactory solution.

At the end of January in 1820 the government was again facing a crisis after George III died and the Prince Regent became George IV. Feeling was running high in the country and in February a conspiracy was hatched to murder Lord Liverpool and his entire cabinet. The assassinations would be carried out at a 'a cabinet dinner' to be held in the home of Lord Harrowby. It became known as the Cato Street Conspiracy (after the locality of the house where the conspirators met). However, it was foiled when a government spy infiltrated the group and passed on information to the authorities. Consequently, on 23 February, instead of the government members they had expected to find, the conspirators found themselves facing a group of Bow Street runners. In the ensuing struggle a Bow Street runner was killed and thirteen conspirators were arrested and charged with high treason. Of these, one was the government spy, who was released; two turned king's evidence resulting in charges against them being dropped. Of the remaining ten, five were transported for life and five were executed. Half an hour after the executions, in front of the large crowd which had gathered to witness them, the five were cut down and beheaded with a small knife to brand them as traitors. The government now hoped that any further thought of rebellion or protest by the 'lower orders' against their lot in life would be firmly squashed. It was not to be the case.

James Wroe, editor of the *Manchester Observer* (co-founded with John Knight, Joseph Johnson and John Saxton as a radical reform newspaper in 1818) had, as mentioned earlier, coined the phrase 'Peterloo', and written several pamphlets bearing that title. Wroe had often been sued for libel for his stances and the authorities were now beyond furious with him for likening the incident on St Peter's Field to the Battle of Waterloo. It gave the whole episode an importance and legitimacy which they felt was not deserved. Consequently, the government undertook repeated prosecutions for 'seditious libel' against Wroe until he was financially ruined, in addition to imprisoning him for six months. The newspaper experienced grave difficulties as a result and finally ceased publication in 1821. The Establishment may have been jubilant at this news, but in reality all they had succeeded in doing was shooting themselves in the foot. The *Manchester Observer* was replaced, in that same year, 1821, by the *Manchester Guardian* (now *The Guardian*). Founded by John Taylor, the *Manchester Guardian* continued the promotion of liberal and radical interests by campaigning vociferously against the Corn Laws. It was published weekly on Saturdays until 1836, when a Wednesday edition was added, and daily from 1855 when stamp duty on newspapers was finally abolished. Today, almost two centuries later, The [*Manchester*] *Guardian* is still a flourishing daily newspaper promoting liberal and radical thinking. However, in the immediate aftermath of Peterloo, the press was muzzled unless it agreed entirely with establishment thinking.

John Tyas, the *Times* correspondent at Peterloo, was arrested along with Henry Hunt but after his release he published what may be the most truthful and sympathetic account of Peterloo. It was over 10,000 words long, but he made the important point that the crowd was peaceful, unarmed, and initially cooperative to the cavalry.

> The Yeomanry Cavalry were seen advancing in a rapid trot to the area: their ranks were in disorder, and on arriving within it, they halted to breathe their horses, and to recover their ranks. A panic seemed to strike the persons at the outskirts of the meeting, who immediately began to scamper in every direction.

> After a moment's pause, the cavalry drew their swords, and brandished them fiercely in the air: upon which Hunt and [Joseph] Johnson desired the multitude to give three cheers, to show the military that they were not to be daunted in the discharge of their duty by their unwelcome presence. This they did, upon which Mr. Hunt again proceeded. This was a mere trick to interrupt the proceedings of the meeting: but he trusted that they would all stand firm.

> He had scarcely said these words, before the Manchester Yeomanry Cavalry rode into the mob, which gave way before them, and directed their course to the cart from which Hunt was speaking. Not a brickbat was thrown at them – not a pistol was fired during this period: all was quiet and orderly, as if the cavalry had been the friends of the multitude and had marched as such into the midst of them.

Henry Hunt and Joseph Johnson were then arrested and jumped down off the hustings. Tyas continues:

> As soon as Hunt and Johnson had jumped from the waggon, a cry was made by the cavalry, 'Have at their flags.' In consequence, they immediately dashed not only at the flags

which were in the waggon, but those which were posted among the crowd, cutting most indiscriminately to the right and to the left in order to get at them. This set the people running in all directions, and it was not till this act had been committed that any brick-bats were hurled at the military. From that moment, the Manchester Yeomanry Cavalry lost all command of temper. A person of the name of Saxton, who is, we believe, the editor of the Manchester Observer, was standing in the cart. Two privates rode up to him. 'There,' said one of them, 'is that villain, Saxton; do you run him through the body?' 'No,' replied the other, 'I had rather not – I leave it to you.' The man immediately made a lunge at Saxton, and it was only by slipping aside that the blow missed his life. As it was, it cut his coat and waistcoat but fortunately did him no other injury … a man within five yards of us in another direction had his nose completely taken off by a blow of a sabre; whilst another was laid prostrate, but whether he was dead or had merely thrown himself down to obtain protection we cannot say. Seeing all this hideous work going on, we felt an alarm which any man may be forgiven for feeling in a similar situation: looking around us, we saw a constable at no great distance, and thinking that our only chance of safety rested in placing ourselves under his protection, we appealed to him for assistance. He immediately took us into custody … just as we came to the house, the constables were conducting Hunt into it, and were treating him in a manner in which they were neither justified by law nor humanity, striking him with their staves on the head.

The Times, 1819

It was Tyas's factual account in all its appalling detail which prompted Percy Bysshe Shelley to write his epic 372 line poem 'The Masque of Anarchy' in 1819, although it was not published until 1832. Three of the quatrains are particularly pertinent:

And if then the tyrants dare
Let them ride among you there
Slash, and stab, and maim and hew;
What they like; that let them do

What is Freedom? Ye can tell
That which Slavery is too well,
For its very name has grown
To an echo of your own

Rise, like lions after slumber
In unvanquishable number!
Shake your chains to earth like dew
Which in sleep had fallen on you:
Ye are many – they are few.

Chapter 6

Repercussions of Peterloo and the Inquest on John Lees

The authorities now faced a difficult situation. There was to be an inquest into the death of John Lees which was going to be problematical in that it might publicly prove what had really happened at Peterloo. It began on 8 September in Oldham. The official coroner was conveniently away so proceedings were organised by an obstructive and officious little clerk rather aptly named Mr Batty, whose favourite method of dealing with any problem was an adjournment. Eventually, after numerous frustrating delays, the coroner, Mr Farrand, returned. He impanelled and swore in a coroner's jury on 25 September. The twelve good men and true included: John Jackson; Thomas Wolfenden; James Coats; George Dixon; Henry Woolstonholme; Thomas Booth; John Key; George Booth; Joseph Dixon; Thomas Jackson; John Newton; John Ogden. There were a large number of witnesses including John Lees' father Robert Lees; Dr Earnshaw, who attended John Lees; Mr Cox the pathologist; Edward Meagher, a trumpeter in the Manchester and Salford Yeomanry; Joseph Chadwick, a local constable and an Oldham hatter; reporters Francis Shaw and James Edwards; and a score of other people who had seen John Lees wounded. The cause of death was given as gangrene, which had set in after the wounds failed to heal properly. One of the witnesses, however, Samuel Davenport, an engraver from South Manchester, was prevented by the coroner from giving evidence of John Lees' wounding. After a series of constant delays and adjournments, the inquest was finally adjourned in early December and never resumed, because the

(*Above*) A group meeting of female reformers in the summer of 1819. A number of such groups were founded in the north west during the months prior to Peterloo and were subject to sarcasm and bitter satire. Here a lone male reporter is supposedly hiding under the table in order to give his colleagues salacious gossip on the inadequacy of females in politics.

(*Below*) A map of St Peter's Field on 16 August 1819, next to St Peter's Church, which stood on the site of the present St Peter's Square tram stop. (*Manchester Libraries, Information and Archives*)

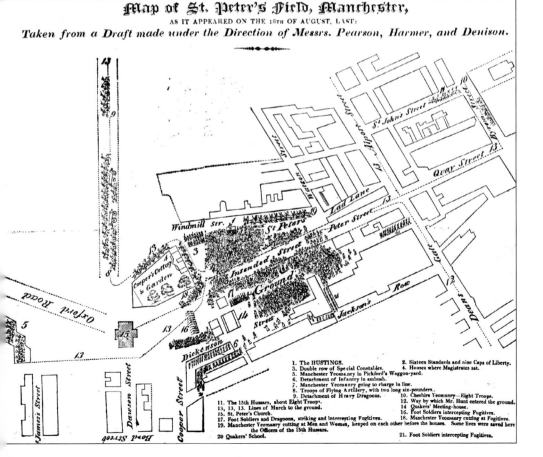

Map of St. Peter's Field, Manchester,

AS IT APPEARED ON THE 16TH OF AUGUST, LAST:

Taken from a Draft made under the Direction of Messrs. Pearson, Harmer, and Denison.

1. The HUSTINGS.
2. Sixteen Standards and nine Caps of Liberty.
3. Double row of Special Constables.
4. Houses where Magistrates sat.
5. Manchester Yeomanry in Pickford's Waggon-yard.
6. Detachment of Infantry in ambush.
7. Manchester Yeomanry going to charge in line.
8. Troops of Flying Artillery, with two long six-pounders.
9. Detachment of Heavy Dragoons.
10. Cheshire Yeomanry—Eight Troops.
11. The 15th Hussars, about Eight Troops.
12. Way by which Mr. Hunt entered the ground.
13, 13, 13. Lines of March to the ground.
14 Quakers' Meeting-house.
15. St. Peter's Church.
16. Foot Soldiers intercepting Fugitives.
17. Foot Soldiers and Dragoons, striking and intercepting Fugitives.
18. Manchester Yeomanry cutting at Fugitives.
19. Manchester Yeomanry cutting at Men and Women, heaped on each other before the houses. Some lives were saved here by the Officers of the 15th Hussars.
20 Quakers' School.
21. Foot Soldiers intercepting Fugitives.

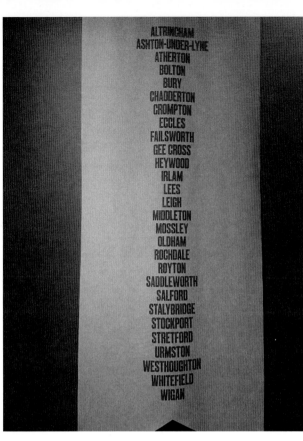

ALTRINCHAM
ASHTON-UNDER-LYNE
ATHERTON
BOLTON
BURY
CHADDERTON
CROMPTON
ECCLES
FAILSWORTH
GEE CROSS
HEYWOOD
IRLAM
LEES
LEIGH
MIDDLETON
MOSSLEY
OLDHAM
ROCHDALE
ROYTON
SADDLEWORTH
SALFORD
STALYBRIDGE
STOCKPORT
STRETFORD
URMSTON
WESTHOUGHTON
WHITEFIELD
WIGAN

(*Left*) A list of the contingents who marched to Peterloo from various north-western towns on 16 August 1819. (*People's History Museum, Manchester*)

(*Below*) Peterloo, St Peter's Place, Manchester, on 16 August 1819 showing the cavalry arriving at the hustings to arrest Henry Hunt. (*Manchester Libraries, Information and Archives*)

(*Above*) Henry Hunt on the hustings with Mary Fildes at Peterloo (originally published by Richard Carlile). Hunt, a well known orator and campaigner for social justice, was due to be the day's chief speaker. (*Manchester Libraries, Information and Archives*)

(*Below*) Manchester 'heroes': the cavalry charge into the crowd, slashing and stabbing at random with their sabres. Women were particularly singled out for attack. (*Manchester Libraries, Information and Archives*)

Meeting dispersal in St Peter's Place as men, women and children flee in terror from the cavalry. (*Manchester Libraries, Information and Archives*)

William Hulton, chief magistrate at Peterloo. Hulton was in Mr Cooper's cottage (on part of the present Midland Hotel site) with fellow magistrates and gave the order for the cavalry to charge. (*Manchester Libraries, Information and Archives*)

'Love conquers Fear': child workers in the mills of Manchester, 1820. The young workers encourage each other as they undertake the dangerous task of crawling beneath fast moving machinery to clean it. (*Manchester Libraries, Information and Archives*)

Silhouette of Henry Hunt, orator at Peterloo. (*Manchester Libraries, Information and Archives*)

Harriet Martineau, 1846. One of the first real 'sociologists', she was disapproved of in Victorian England due to her criticism of slavery and support for female suffrage. (*Manchester Libraries, Information and Archives*)

(*Above*) Queen Victoria and Prince Albert, 1850. The queen strongly disapproved of female suffrage, but was sympathetic towards some of the social injustices suffered by women. (*Manchester Libraries, Information and Archives*)

(*Right*) Unknown lady wearing a crinoline dress, c.1866. Crinoline wearers were accident prone and the crinolines themselves were a terrible fire risk, but male peer pressure insisted that women should continue to wear them.

Josephine Butler, 1876. A supporter of female suffrage and legal recognition of married women, Butler campaigned hard against child prostitution and the indignities of the Contagious Diseases [STDs] Act. (*Manchester Libraries, Information and Archives*)

William Ewart Gladstone, 1878. Originally a Conservative MP, he became a Liberal prime minister and fought hard for electoral reform after being impressed by the working classes. (*Manchester Libraries, Information and Archives*)

(*Above*) Peterloo veterans photographed by John Birch in 1884. Having participated at Peterloo in 1819, they now took part in the Great Reform Demonstration in 1884, under the same banner which they had marched with at Peterloo. (*Manchester Libraries, Information and Archives*)

(*Right*) Lydia Becker, 1890. Becker was an academic who started the female suffrage movement in Manchester in 1868 and became a role model for Emmeline Pankhurst. Her campaigning gained women the vote on the Isle of Man in 1881. (*Manchester Libraries, Information and Archives*)

(*Above*) The backs of tenement buildings in Potts Street, Ancoats, in 1899. A good example of the overcrowded and often insanitary conditions in which mill workers and their families were forced to live. (*Manchester Libraries, Information and Archives*)

(*Below*) Brazil Mill, Commercial Street, Manchester, 1896. The unguarded machinery and cramped conditions meant accidents were common. Unguarded machinery was still used in Ancoats during the 1960s. (*Manchester Libraries, Information and Archives*)

(*Above*) Samuel Bamford's cottage in 1900, now in Greater Manchester. Samuel Bamford led the Middleton contingent at Peterloo and later wrote his political memoirs. (*Manchester Libraries, Information and Archives*)

(*Below*) Emmeline Pankhurst and her daughters in Manchester, 1910. Emmeline (left) led the militant WSPU's fight for female suffrage, aided by Christabel (centre), who shared her mother's beliefs. Sylvia (right) was a socialist and pacifist who greatly irritated her mother and sister. After giving birth to an illegitimate son, she emigrated to Addis Ababa. (*Manchester Libraries, Information and Archives*)

Statue of suffragette Annie Kenney outside Oldham Town Hall. A mill girl, self-educated and a hard worker, she helped to found the WSPU in 1903 and was the only working class woman allowed in the hierarchy of the organisation.

St. Peter's Cross, Manchester. 84.

Cross on the site of the former St Peter's Church, Manchester, in 1913. The cross stands opposite the entrance to Central Library and marks the approximate site of the path leading to the front of the church. Beneath the pavements nearby are buried catacombs, including the tomb of Hugh Birley, who led the cavalry charge at Peterloo.

(*Above*) Female LNWR (London and North Western Railway) staff in Manchester, 1917, demonstrating that they could do the job of any man during the Great War. (*Manchester Libraries, Information and Archives*)

(*Below*) Belgian GCR (Great Central Railway) drayman with a female porter in Manchester, 1917. The willingness, adaptability and hard work of females during the Great War eventually won them the vote in 1918. (*Manchester Libraries, Information and Archives*)

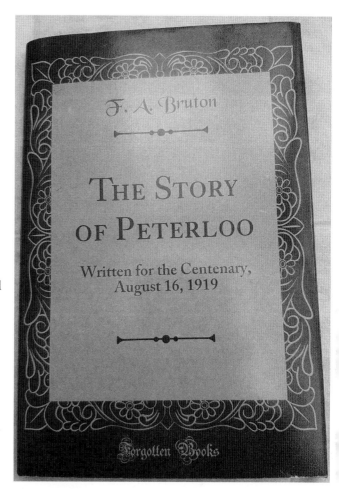

(*Right*) This commemorative booklet, written by a Manchester Grammar School teacher, was the sole marker of the centenary of Peterloo in August 1919.

(*Below*) The covered linkway between Central Library and Town Hall includes name tiles on the floor commemorating the Peterloo victims. Sarah Jones was beaten around the head with a truncheon and disabled.

(*Left*) A memorial plaque to Peterloo on the wall of the former Free Trade Hall (now the Radisson Blu Hotel), where Lydia Becket launched the fight for female suffrage. The site was formerly part of St Peter's Field.

(*Below*) Peterloo memorial, designed by Turner prize winning artist Jeremy Deller, at Manchester Central Station, commemorating the bi-centenary of Peterloo in 2019. Names of those killed and injured are inscribed around the circumference of each circular block.

authorities did not want the full facts known. By then, however, it was accepted that there had been deaths and injuries and an official compensation scheme was set up. The compensation book, detailing names, addresses, ages and occupations of those killed or injured, as well as details of their injuries or cause of death, and the amounts of individual compensation paid, survives, and Michael Bush has published an account and complete list of names in his excellent book *The Casualties of Peterloo* (2007). Compensation paid was often scant, but many victims, even the children, desperately tried to hide their injuries and did not dare to claim for fear either of the authorities taking punitive action, or that they would lose their jobs. In addition, those leading the meeting had all been jailed. By this time there was a widespread feeling that the Peterloo meeting was a complete failure. At great personal cost, nothing had been achieved, and the leaders were all in jail. Henry Hunt was serving 2½ years in Ilchester prison. Joseph Johnson, Samuel Bamforth and Joseph Healey had all been sentenced to a year's imprisonment.

Despite Establishment views of radical reform and the Peterloo episode, however, there was a great deal of public sympathy and support. The government had refused to hold either a public or governmental enquiry. They simply condemned the meeting as an act of treason and one magistrate thought that radical and reforming perpetrators should be hanged. The evidence of several eye-witnesses, such as that of Elizabeth Farren and Margaret Goodwin who could name the troopers who attacked them, was simply dismissed. Joseph Nadin was also called, but he either denied or contradicted the evidence which had been given. He was believed because he was deputy chief constable, but he was also believed because of the views of the Establishment. Just a month after Peterloo a magistrate had made clear the official view of Peterloo, telling the accused person facing him that 'I believe you are a downright blackguard reformer. Some of you reformers ought to be hanged, and some of you are sure to be hanged – the rope is already around your necks' (*The Peterloo Massacre*, Ruth Nadin, 2008).

The inquest hearing on John Lees had been a farce and many felt that the authorities had gone too far. It simply wasn't done for cavalry to charge into a crowd of their own unarmed people, or to indiscriminately try to hack terrified women and children to pieces. Although there were far more men than women at Peterloo, in recent times it has been worked out that a far higher proportion of women were attacked than their male counterparts. Indeed, it was said at the time that women were singled out 'to teach them a lesson'. There were '654 recorded casualties, of whom 168 were women. Four died either on St Peter's Field or afterwards as a result of their wounds.'

It has been estimated that less than 12 per cent of the crowd was made up of females, but almost 25 per cent of the casualties were female, suggesting that women were at significantly greater risk of injury than men by a factor of almost 3:1. If the intention at Peterloo had been to 'teach women a lesson', and cow them into submission, this intention backfired spectacularly because it not only gained public sympathy, it also encouraged female radicals and reformers to fight even harder for justice. The Yeomanry who had wounded them were never officially punished, but many were shamed and shunned by their own communities. There were large numbers of donations for those hurt at Peterloo in addition to the scant sums paid by the authorities. With the Six Acts, Lord Liverpool's Conservative government had cracked down on freedom of speech, freedom of the press and freedom to hold meetings, but they could not quench the radical and rebellious spirit, and the Six Acts were generally considered to be an over-reaction. Percy Byshhe Shelley, in Italy at the time of the Peterloo massacre, had written 'The Masque of Anarchy' encouraging radicals and reformers, 'a stabbed and starved people', to 'rise like lions from slumber, in unvanquishable number' and at around the same time William Hone, a satirist with a clever turn of phrase, wrote 'The Political House that Jack Built':

> Who cursed the day wherein they were born
> On account of taxation too great to be borne
> And pray for relief from night to morn
> Who, in vain, petition in very form.
> Who, peaceably meeting to ask for Reform,
> Were sabred by Yeoman Cavalry ...

Chapter 7

The *Manchester Comet* and the Situation of Women After Peterloo

Newspapers which followed and complemented government guidelines were, however, allowed to be published. The *Manchester Comet*, of which only one issue was ever published (on 30 October 1822), was such a newspaper. It was stinging in its ridicule and dismissal of radical thought or reform in general, and criticised proposed female rights in particular. In many respects it was a nasty little piece of work, a vitriolic mixture of extreme views and bitter humour at its very worst.

Long before Peterloo there had been letters written to various local Manchester newspapers on the subject of female reformers, decrying radical reformers and the notion that women might have any kind of rights, let alone the right to vote. Now the *Manchester Comet* entered the fray and published its own repressive and conservative opinions on female involvement in politics and Peterloo.

> But the most disgusting, and to a reflecting mind the most painful part of the proceedings of the self-styled reformists, is the introduction of females as actors at their clubs and public meetings. Good God! How abhorrent is it that from retiring modesty which ought to be the boast of every English woman, for them to join in the noisy brawls of politics; how painful to behold them assembled at the ale house or the club room neglecting those near and sacred duties which their situations as daughters, as wives, or as mothers, impose upon them. We know they are suffering, and we lament their distress; but they

may be assured that neither aping those proceedings of men which they cannot imitate, nor manufacturing caps of liberty will tend to alleviate their distress. The fulfilment of these private duties which our individual situation in life imposes upon each of us, is of far more imperative obligation than any of those which are merely political; and this applies much more strongly to females than even to men. The order and constitution of society marks them for domestic employment and domestic duties, and they cannot depart from that line which nature herself has pointed out for them, without an absolute forfeiture of their respectability and usefulness …

Usefulness, as one critic pointed out, was the key word here. What was really wrong, was that large numbers of pompous, self-important males wanted lifelong mothers and were intent on turning marriage into little more than legalised prostitution and slavery. Writers like Jane Austen and Anne Brontë recognised this fact in their books, and a letter written by Caroline Norton, the desperate wife of one George Norton, during the 1830s/1840s illustrates the point well. His treatment of his wife became a cause célèbre. Caroline wrote many letters to the queen pleading her case, and made a number of valid points concerning the injustices meted out to women.

'a married woman has no legal existence in England … [and] she has no possessions'

'an English wife cannot make a will … the law gives what she has to her husband'

'an English wife cannot legally claim her own earnings'

'an English wife may not leave her husband's house' (i.e. leave home) 'if her husband takes proceedings for divorce she is not allowed to defend herself'

'if an English wife is guilty of infidelity her husband can divorce her … but she cannot divorce her husband (for the same reason)'

'she cannot prosecute for libel'

'she cannot sign a lease, or transact responsible business'

Due largely to Caroline Norton's campaigning, the Custody of Infants Act 1839 was passed in Parliament and included many of her recommendations. It was generally acknowledged that there had been need for reform because previously, custody of children in divorce cases was almost always awarded to the father and the mother might never see them again. As a result of the new Act, mothers could petition for custody of their children up to the age of 7 and for access to older children. This helped ease the heartbreak of mothers separated from their young children.

Despite her ordeals, Caroline Norton, unlike many other women, did not suffer the worst fate which could have befallen her.

During the eighteenth and nineteenth centuries it was considered acceptable to commit 'inconvenient women' (as they were termed) to mental asylums for life. 'Inconvenient women' were usually unwanted spouses or maiden aunts; sometimes mothers of illegitimate children. Most of these unfortunate cases were members of upper-class families, partly due to the cost of maintenance, but also due to the fact that asylums were often encouraged to keep patients as a result of 'charitable donations' made by their families to ensure that certain women should remain incarcerated, despite the fact there was little reason for many of them not to be discharged. The case of Lady Harriet Mordaunt became a cause célèbre in 1870, just ten years after Coventry Patmore had completed his poem 'The Angel in the House'. Harriet Mordaunt was said to have enjoyed flirtations and affairs with other men when her husband, Sir Charles Mordaunt, was away on business or fishing trips. It was considered perfectly acceptable for men to indulge in this way, but in a woman it was considered to be 'very fragile virtue'. Lady Harriet eventually gave birth to a baby daughter. The baby was at first thought to be blind, but although this turned out not to be the case, it prompted Lady Harriet to confess that her baby was illegitimate in case a sexually transmitted disease had caused the baby's ailment, and Sir Charles sued for divorce. In the days following the birth, Lady Harriet had 'behaved nervously and erratically', and she may have been suffering from post-natal depression. Her family then claimed she was insane because insanity was not grounds for divorce, and this would prevent Sir Charles' divorce petition from being successful. The subsequent court hearing determined she was suffering from 'puerperal mania', she was declared insane and committed to an asylum. Subsequently, however, it emerged that Lady Harriet's real sin had been a lack of discretion. The Prince of Wales (who later became Edward VII) had become implicated as one of those with whom she had supposedly enjoyed a brief affair and it was deemed necessary, according to the social rules of the day, to 'silence her'. Her 'punishment' for being 'mad and bad' was to be incarcerated in asylums for the rest of her life until she died in 1906. Sir Charles eventually obtained his divorce on grounds of her adultery and remarried. Those with whom she had enjoyed her brief flings were not made to suffer in any way, and it was Lady Harriet alone who bore the brunt and the punishment for her brief liaisons. The only person to show any sadness and concern over the whole matter was Princess Alexandra, wife of the future Edward VII.

The *Comet* continued on its tirades, however. The by-line of the newspaper was 'A Rap at Radicals'. The newspaper felt that the Whigs (Liberals) were to blame for everything. There were verbal attacks and accusations of 'fake news'. The radicals had 'opened Pandora's box', and according to the *Comet*: 'our justly beloved country is now in a state of happiness and comparative affluence ... plenty at home, peace and respect, and admiration of her gigantic energies abroad place her at once on a higher pinnacle than any nation.'

Although radically minded individuals pointed out that much of the Empire-building was done through slavery, child labour, invasion and looting of other countries, appalling living, working and dying conditions for many, if not most, of the population in the millscapes, maltreatment of the Irish and no rights at all for females, the *Comet* had carried on regardless; 'the arch enemies of our unrivalled constitution, like the unrivalled friend of Scripture, are constantly on the alert, seeking whom they may devour' and then continued:

'It shall be our place to take the place of public sentinels, and with the eye of the lynx, the perseverance of the mole, and the cunning of the fox, endeavour to guard her against the ungrateful machinations of her domestic foes.' Before threatening 'HUNT will be HUNTed!'

A long, bitter, ironic satire on a meeting of female radicals portrays them as drunks with heavy coarse sexual innuendo and no mention of real problems, lack of rights, or female issues; although the paper was actually just reflecting much of society's general dislike and dismissal of its female sex at that time. Hannah Saxon, wife of Joseph Saxon (one of Hunt's hustings supporters at Peterloo) was associated with a long spiel on 'breakfast powders' and 'burnt oatmeal', and she is depicted in a cartoon as dancing drunkenly, almost lewdly, on a table at the meeting. A fictional political commentator character named 'Goose-tongue-Bury', is a witty play on Glastonbury and refers to 'spiritual' as being either religious or alcoholic; but, of course, in female radical reformers it could only be alcoholic.

Chapter 8

Electoral Reform … but Not for Women

In the immediate aftermath of Peterloo there was a general feeling of despondency and failure. Those who took part felt they had not achieved anything that they had wanted, and that it had all been at terrible personal and violent cost. To add insult to injury the Six Acts had further curtailed what few freedoms they did have. For a while the situation seemed hopeless and the entitled moneyed classes appeared to have simply tightened their stranglehold on worker's rights, on the prices they could obtain for their labour, on social and economic conditions and, at times, on their personal liberties. It was a difficult time, but despite the general depression and the misgivings of those who had suffered at Peterloo and afterwards, it was not the end of the quest for reform. The quest was, in fact, far from over. Peterloo had only been the beginning. Throughout the 1820s the ideas of one man, one vote, equal size of parliamentary boroughs and a secret ballot, were kept alive and carefully nurtured. Memories of the French Revolution were still strong, and this meant that these issues did get some discussion time in Parliament, but George IV and the Tory government were not at all sympathetic, especially Lord Sidmouth, although he had retired as home secretary in 1821. The prime minister, Lord Liverpool, was also vocal in his opposition.

The radical idea of female suffrage was first raised in 1817 by a man, Jeremy Bentham, an English philosopher and social reformer, when he published his 'Plan of Parliamentary Reform'. Although working-class women remained doubtful that female suffrage would ever be granted, they still believed fervently in the principle and, at the end of November 1819, the Female Reformers of Manchester issued an address to William Cobbett, praising his endeavours on behalf of the reform movement and thanking him for his support.

James Mill, a Scottish economist and the father of John Stuart Mill, largely dismissed the idea of female suffrage in 1825 when he stated that,

> all those individuals whose interests are indisputably included in those of other individuals may be struck off without any inconvenience ... in this light women may also be regarded, the interests of almost all of whom are involved in that of their fathers or that of their husbands.

This provoked a response from a couple named William Thompson, an Irish social reformer, and Anna Wheeler, an Irish writer who supported female suffrage, when they published a book with the catchy title 'An appeal of one half of the human race, women, against the pretensions of the other half, men, to retain them in political, and thence in civil and domestic slavery: in reply to Mr Mills' celebrated "Article on Government"'. The title may have been ponderous, but the theme was not.

The first breakthrough finally came in 1830. George IV (formerly the Prince Regent) died and his brother, William IV, 'the 'sailor king', came to the throne. William was far less pompous and extravagant than his brother, albeit he had strongly conservative attitudes. George's death dissolved Parliament automatically by law and forced a general election. Although the Tories won a majority of the seats the party was divided, particularly over the question of electoral reform, which had been a major campaigning issue in the election. Support for electoral reform in the country was now quite strong and well supported by local political unions of both working and middle classes, as well as by the Whigs. Support for the prime minister, the Duke of Wellington, even from his own party, was weak. He was strongly opposed to any kind of electoral reform and he gave a long-winded third-party style speech in the Commons on the subject.

> He was fully convinced that the country possessed, at the present moment, a legislature which answered all the good purposes of legislation, and this to a greater degree than any legislature ever had answered, in any country whatever. He would go further and say that the legislature and system of representation possessed the full and entire confidence of the country. […] He would go still further, and say, that if at the present moment he had imposed upon him the duty of forming a legislature for any country […] he did not mean to assert that he could form such a legislature as they possessed now, for the nature of man was incapable of reaching such excellence at once. […] As long as he held any station in the government of the country, he should always feel it his duty to resist [reform] measures, when proposed by others.

This did not go down well, even with the Tories, and after a vote of no confidence, he resigned at the end of November 1830. He was succeeded by the Whig reformer, Charles Grey, whose first pledge was to carry out electoral reform.

Chapter 9

The First (Great) Reform Act 1832

The Whigs introduced the First Reform Bill of major parliamentary reforms in March 1831 which disenfranchised sixty of the smallest boroughs and reduced the representation of another forty-seven. Some seats were abolished, while others were redistributed to London, Manchester, Leeds, other large cities and the counties. On the second reading, however, the Bill was passed by only one vote, and there were still bitter divisions in the Commons. Lord Sidmouth had retained his absolute opposition to electoral reform, and there were many who agreed with him. Grey then decided, because electoral reform was so important and so long overdue, to dissolve Parliament and call a general election. The Whigs won with an overwhelming majority and in July the Bill was re-introduced to the Commons as a Second Reform Bill. It was finally passed in September by a majority of 100, but they had reckoned without the House of Lords. The Lords had no intention of letting working-class upstarts have any say in the important business of running the country if they could possibly help it and rejected the Bill. This caused serious civil unrest with riots up and down the country, notably in Bristol where the Council House was burned down; Nottingham where the Castle was attacked in an echo of the Robin Hood legend; in Derby where the Industrial Revolution had really begun, and in Dorset, Leicestershire and Somerset.

Different local groups coalesced into a National Political Union to put further pressure on the government. A Third Reform Bill was introduced in December after William IV had been asked to prorogue Parliament because the same Bill could not be introduced twice in the same session. The main difference between this Bill and the others was that it no longer recommended a reduction of seats in the House of Commons. This Bill passed with a larger majority and was sent to the Lords. This time, rather than rejection, the Lords decided on delay through extended discussion of the clauses disenfranchising rotten boroughs. The Cabinet advised the king to create a number of new peerages for pro-reformers to push the Bill through the Lords. William IV refused and Grey resigned. The king then invited the Duke of Wellington to form a government. The country was furious. The National Political Union sent angry petitions to the Commons. There was a run on the banks in protest and calls for the abolition of both the Lords and the monarchy. Despite promising moderate political reform, Wellington was unable to form a government and the king was left with no choice but to recall Charles Grey. William IV eventually consented to create new Whig peers but Wellington, who was no fool, had already quietly advised the Lords not to resist further for fear of the consequences, and the Bill finally received Royal Assent on 7 June 1832.

The new Act made great changes to the electoral system. There were 203 boroughs in England and fifty-six of the smallest were abolished, another thirty lost one of their two MPs, while Weymouth and Melcombe Regis lost two of their four MPs. The Act also created 130 new seats, of which half were new county seats and half were new borough seats. The franchise was extended, but for males only and with a wealth of complicated conditions involving rents, properties, freeholds and leaseholds, and there was still the stumbling block of voters needing to live in properties worth at least £10 per year, which excluded most of the working class. An annual voter registration system was also instigated. Women did not feature in these reforms at all. Although this had been expected, there were still strong feelings among women of resentment and exclusion; especially for working-class women. The Industrial Revolution had taken them out of their homes and into the mills where they worked alongside their menfolk for long hours and lesser wages before going home to undertake the domestic duties of cooking, cleaning and caring for their children. Out of the sheer injustices of this system the female suffrage movement was born just over twenty years later and would claim equal rights for women and eventually ensure that all women, as well as men, had the vote. Basically, it was mainly middle-class males who benefited in terms of the franchise from the Reform Act of 1832 and, in effect, the upper classes remained firmly in charge with the exclusion of most of the population from the franchise still valid, which led to the formation of the Chartist movement. Nevertheless, the journey along the path to universal suffrage had finally begun.

Chapter 10

Chartism and the Women Who Supported it

The Chartist Movement, initiated by the unfulfilled demands of Peterloo for a fairer franchise, began in the aftermath of the 1832 Reform Act and came to prominence in the years 1836–1848. It was a working–class movement whose aim was to obtain further political rights for the working classes and which took its name from the People's Charter, drawn up by its members. There was a great deal of disappointment that the 1832 Act had failed to remove the property qualification for voting which meant that most of the working classes remained excluded from the franchise. What came to be known as the People's Charter was initiated by the London Working Men's Association (LWMA) founded by William Lovett, Henry Hetherington, John Cleeve, Henry Vincent, John Roebuck and James Weston. Francis Place was a member of the LWMA, and in 1838, together with William Lovett, he drew up the first draft of the People's Charter. There were six main points:

- A vote for all males over the age of 21
- A secret ballot
- No property qualifications for becoming an MP
- Payment of MPs as for any other job
- Electoral districts of equal size
- Annual elections for Parliament

Many of the Chartist associations were centred in the industrial areas such as North West and North East England; the Potteries; the Black Country and the South Wales valleys. The Leeds representative of the LWMA was Feargus O'Connor who, in 1837, founded a radical newspaper, the *Northern Star*, in the city. He had become well known as a Chartist orator, working hard to promote the Peoples' Charter.

Women were well aware of the People's Charter's limitations since they were not mentioned, but many argued that if all males got the vote and there was a relaxation of property qualifications, it would enable greater political involvement for men and strengthen the case for females having similar involvement as well as the vote. Many male Chartists believed in the vote for women, but many did not, so most large towns also had female Chartist associations, and the East London Female Patriotic Association voiced the general aim succinctly in their Objectives published in 1839:

> '[we want] to unite with our sisters in the country, and to use our best endeavours to assist our brethren in attaining universal suffrage'.

There were several female Chartist associations, notably in Bradford, Cheltenham, Manchester, Stockport, Leicester, Nottingham, Ashton, Carlisle, Loughborough, Sheffield, Todmorden, Rochdale and Halifax. Female Chartist associations were usually quite large and active. A Birmingham group had over 3,000 female members. The Chartist group in Hyde (Cheshire) had 300 male and 200 female members and the *Northern Star* quoted one of the male members who stated that 'the women were the better men'.

Mary Fildes had been on the hustings at Peterloo with Henry Hunt and she became active in the early Chartist movement, remaining so throughout the 1830s and the early 1840s. In 1833 she helped to establish the Female Political Union of the Working Classes.

Elizabeth Hanson formed a 'female radical association' in 1838 in Elland, near Leeds and became a popular Chartist orator, to 'co-operate with our husbands and sons in their great work of regeneration'. Her husband, Abram Hanson, an important local Chartist leader in the Leeds area, paid tribute to the importance of 'the women who are the best politicians, the best revolutionists, and the best political economists ... should the men fail in their allegiance the women of Elland, who had sworn not to breed slaves, had registered a vow to do the work of men and women.' (*Northern Star* 1838)

Mary Anne Walker was a mysterious figure who appeared briefly on the stage of Chartist history in 1842 and disappeared about a year afterwards. She helped Susanna Inge form the Female Chartist Association and she was fond of promoting both the organisation and herself. Almost nothing is known about her, but it would appear that she lived in the London/Kent area and *The Times* described her as 'tall and of prepossessing countenance and figure, with much of grace and dignity of contour in her manner and action', while the *Northern Star* waxed lyrical over her physical charms,

> she was dressed in mourning ... for the death of her father of whom she had not been many months bereaved ... the body of her dress was partial and becomingly low, displaying a very graceful bust ... to set off ... a figure and form of interesting proportions ... she appeared more than usually wan ... the effect ... of her anxiety to convey satisfaction to her audience ... she wore a light sort of crepe scarf, or negligee, attached gracefully ... to her arms ... and ... a jet necklace suspending a cross ... adorned her bosom.

Susanna Inge, a Folkestone woman born and bred and a member of London Female Radical Association, became a leading voice in the female Chartist movement. In the summer of 1842, the *Northern Star* published an article about her in which she was quoted as saying 'as civilisation advances man becomes more inclined to place woman on an equality with himself and ... her condition is considerably improved'. Later that year she and Mary Ann Walker, both of whom took up column inches of print in the *Northern Star*, formed a Female Chartist

Movement despite considerable criticism from male Chartists, one of whom was unwise enough to say that he 'did not consider that nature had intended women to partake of political rights … women were more happy in the peacefulness and usefulness of the domestic hearth'. In this view he was joined by Feargus O'Connor, who stated that women's role in life 'was to be a housewife to prepare meals, to wash, to brew, and look after my comforts, and the education of my children'. Their views of women simply as useful servile objects who existed only to mother men enraged thousands of women, not least Susanna Inge, and she split with Feargus O'Connor over his ideas on the status of women. However, it was not so much his views on the role of women in life which caused the split, but the fact that he also believed in militant action to attain his objectives and he had become the leader of the Physical Force Chartists. She finally left the Chartist movement in February 1843 after a serious dispute with Mary Ann Walker, who also then disappeared into history sometime in the summer of 1843.

For women there were additional issues to be considered. They wanted their husbands and sons to be able to earn decent wages, 'a fair day's pay for a fair day's work', so that they could support their families without their women and children being forced to work long hours outside the home as well as in it. Elizabeth Peace, one of the more vocal female Chartists stated that,

> the grand principle of the natural equality of man – a principle alas almost buried, in the land, beneath the rubbish of an hereditary aristocracy and the force of a State religion … working people are driven almost to desperation by those who consider they are but chattels made to minister to their luxury and add to their wealth.

The Corn Laws were still in operation, bread prices remained high, there was a great deal of hunger and poverty, all of which the wealthier sections of society tended to blame on those who were suffering, arguing that they simply weren't working hard enough and any concessions would only cause 'laissez faire' attitudes. The poor were all forced to pay taxes and other dues to the government and other various authorities, but had absolutely no say in who would be elected or who would set the amounts and collect these monies. This had been the cry at Peterloo, alongside pleas for a fair and democratic parliamentary system. Emma Miles, a 'she-orator' (as speakers of the female Chartists were known) said that she did not doubt that one day Chartism would be successful but 'it would not be granted by justice … it must be extorted from the fears of their oppressors'.

A major figure in the female Chartist movement was Anne Knight; she was a keen advocate of women's rights to which, she felt, not enough attention was being paid by the Chartists, demanding: 'Can man be free if woman be a slave?' In 1848 she became briefly involved in European politics when she criticised the French government for a decree which prohibited women from forming clubs or attending the meetings of associations. The following year she met Richard Cobden but was disappointed by his lack of enthusiasm for women's rights. In 1851 she established the Sheffield Female Political Association, which later that year published 'An Address to the Women of England'. It was the first English petition demanding female suffrage. In 1852 she complained that she was 'forbidden to vote for the man who inflicts the laws I am compelled to obey – the taxes I am compelled to pay … taxation without representation is tyranny', echoing perfectly the feelings of the women at Peterloo and those who supported the Chartist movement of the 1830s and 1840s.

Chapter 11

Political Changes 1830s – 1850s

After the passing of the Great Reform Act of 1832, and amid a good deal of squabbling over the question of Catholic emancipation, Sir Robert Peel, who had introduced the first police force (known as Peelers or Bobbies) in 1829 to assist in keeping public law and order, now set about reinventing the Tory Party. He laid out the Tamworth Manifesto of Conservative principles in 1834 and the old Tory party slowly began to metamorphose into the modern Conservative Party (still nicknamed the Tories).

Adding insult to injury after the Great Reform Act, and causing massive anxiety, was the Poor Law Amendments Act. It was not a direct result of Peterloo but may have been exacerbated by the financial situation of many in the cotton industry during and after Peterloo. The Whig government of Earl Grey, which had been so economical in the extending of the franchise in 1832, had set up a Commission in 1833 to examine how the Poor Law worked in detail. The Commission made a number of recommendations which resulted in the Poor Law Amendment Act being passed in 1834. Some conditions were draconian.

- No able-bodied person was to receive any assistance or financial relief whatsoever except through the means of a workhouse.
- Conditions in the workhouses were to be mean, harsh and Spartan in order to deter people from seeking help.
- A workhouse was to be built in every parish or union of parishes.
- Ratepayers in each parish or union had to appoint a Board of Guardians to administer the workhouse and collect the Poor Rate.

- 'Out relief' (the practice of topping up low earnings or giving financial assistance to the unemployed) was to be abolished, and future relief was to be given only in workhouses where conditions would be so harsh that they would be a deterrent.
- Different classes of paupers were to be segregated and men and women were to be separated even if married.
- Mothers of illegitimate children were to receive much less support and the Poor Law authorities were to no longer help with tracking down the fathers of the children and obtaining financial support from them in an attempt to reduce illegitimate births.
- Poor Law unions were to standardise their treatment of paupers, according to Bentham's theory of utilitarianism, so that paupers would not travel round to obtain relief from workhouses with more favourable conditions.

A Central Poor Law Commission would be appointed by the government to supervise the implementation of the Amendment Act nationally. In 1832, a Royal Commission had recommended sweeping changes in how the Poor Law was administered. There was no general welfare system and those who were unemployed or earned low wages (agricultural labourers were badly paid), or who were too young, too old or too infirm to work, could apply for Poor Law relief. The generally held Malthusian view among wealthier folk was that it was poor people's fault that they were poor, and to offer any financial help was tantamount to encouraging idleness and indolence and would allow the lower classes to breed in larger numbers.

The Poor Law Amendment Act, full of draconian edicts, was passed in 1834 and caused an outcry everywhere. There was immediate and fierce resistance in Manchester to the Poor Law Amendment because the cotton trade had periodic recessions. Workers were often on short time, and 'out-relief' was given to supplement lost wages. The situation affected both male and female workers, but women earned lower wages and thus tended to suffer more. Families were forcibly separated to live in different workhouses in spartan conditions. William Cobbett also objected vociferously to the terms of the Act. He criticised the separation of families in this way and the insistence that workhouse inmates should be forced to wear uniform clothing or special badges. The Act neatly absolved anyone having to help, or even consider, those who had no means of income either through unemployment, age, family circumstances, or absolute poverty. Twelve-hour 'working' days, scant food rations, insufficient bedding and zero comforts were the order of life in the workhouse and many died. Not that the middle or upper classes much cared generally, because it was, as far as they were concerned, the fault of the poor that they were poor. Novelists like Elizabeth Gaskell, who picked up on the horrors of working in the millscapes, or Charles Dickens who recorded so bluntly the poverty and squalor of Victorian England, were heavily criticised by their peers. It was, after all, the time of the glorious British Empire. The country was innovative, wealthy and powerful. Details of workers' hardships and deprivations were regarded as quite irrelevant by many, but never by working-class women who were the most likely to suffer.

Three major petitions containing the six points of Chartism were presented to the government in 1839, 1842 and 1848, but were all rejected in turn. 1.3 million people signed the first petition presented to the House of Commons in 1839, but MPs voted not to hear the petitioners who were then summarily dismissed. This caused great anger and demonstrations, but the Chartists vowed to continue. In 1842 over 3 million people signed the petition, which included the Chartists' original six demands, and also complaints about factory conditions, the Poor Law and 'the unconstitutional police force'. Again it was rejected with a large majority by Parliament. The *Northern Star* commented angrily:

> Three and half millions have quietly, orderly, soberly, peaceably but firmly asked of their rulers to do justice; and their rulers have turned a deaf ear to that protest. Three and a half millions

of people have asked permission to detail their wrongs, and enforce their claims for RIGHT, and the 'House' has resolved they should not be heard! Three and a half millions of the slave-class have holden out the olive branch of peace to the enfranchised and privileged classes and sought for a firm and compact union, on the principle of EQUALITY BEFORE THE LAW; and the enfranchised and privileged have refused to enter into a treaty! The same class is to be a slave class still. The mark and brand of inferiority is not to be removed. The assumption of inferiority is still to be maintained. The people are not to be free.

There was a financial depression in 1842 which led to a wave of strikes in the industrial districts and some violent disturbances. Notable among them were the 'Plug Riots', so called because textile workers removed the boiler plugs from the steam engines powering the mills and manufactories. Trade Union leaders in Manchester also linked the strikes to calls for female suffrage. Although support for Chartism increased during times of economic hardship the Chartist movement was generally peaceful not militant. Although there were civil disturbances during the Chartist years, these were mainly linked to demands for 'a fair day's pay for a fair day's work', and not to the case made by the Chartists. However, the voices of the Chartists got caught up in all the unrest and the demand for the People's Charter was made alongside the demands for restoration or increase of wages. Many Chartists insisted their movement was a peaceful one, but there were those who supported the 'Physical Force' element of the Chartists and this earned them a headline in the *Leeds Mercury* of 'The Chartist Insurrection', which did little for their cause. The government promptly arrested a number of Chartist leaders, although most subsequent prosecutions failed, and none were convicted of any serious charge. Chartists continued their activities, however, and began standing as MPs in elections, but ironically, the only Chartist to become an MP was Feargus O'Connor, who was elected as the Member for Nottingham, and he believed in militancy.

By the mid-1840s Sir Robert Peel, along with many senior Conservatives had begun to favour the repeal of the Corn Laws which had been high on the agenda of Peterloo. This was furiously opposed by members of rural and farming constituencies who were led by Benjamin Disraeli and the Earl of Derby. They argued that the price of corn must be maintained for the benefit of landowners, despite poor harvests and much hunger among the poor. In 1846, the Corn Laws were finally repealed, despite much angst on the part of this opposition who then joined forces with the Whigs to overthrow Peel's government.

The Whigs had evolved from more liberally minded members of the aristocracy than the Tories. Earl Grey, who had masterminded the Great Reform Bill of 1832 was a Whig; so too was Lord Melbourne (prime minister during Victoria's first years as queen) and latterly, Lord Palmerston, more noted as a foreign secretary than as a prime minister, although he oversaw the passing of the Matrimonial Causes Act 1857, which made it possible for civil courts rather than ecclesiastical courts to grant divorces.

Divorce was still easier for men. 'A husband could petition for divorce on the sole grounds that his wife had committed adultery; but a wife could only petition for a divorce based on adultery combined with other offences such as incest, cruelty, bigamy, desertion.' It did allow legal separation, however, by either husband or wife on grounds of adultery, cruelty, or desertion.

By 1839, the Whig Party was evolving into a more liberal party with a broader spectrum. John Bright and Richard Cobden, who favoured social reform, personal liberty and free trade, and who led the Anti-Corn Laws League, were radicals representing newly enfranchised manufacturing constituencies. They and their followers shaped the form and policies of what became the modern Liberal Party, now known as the Lib Dems. The two greatest Liberal prime ministers would be W.E. Gladstone and David Lloyd George.

1848 was the 'Year of Revolution', known as the People's Spring or the Spring of Nations, in Europe. A number of countries were involved including, among others, Italy, France, Germany, Denmark, Hungary, Sweden, Switzerland, Poland, Romania, Belgium, Ireland and Spain. Technological changes occasioned by the Industrial Revolution; long hours; low wages; poor housing; high prices for food and rents; increased taxation; bad harvests in 1846; the potato blight of 1846–47 (responsible for the Irish potato famine); radical thought and reforms, were all contributory factors. In Britain, Irish Chartist, Feargus O'Connor, was an active MP and the Chartists had gained in momentum and popularity. In April of that year it was decided to convene a large public meeting on Kennington Common to deliver a third petition to Parliament. This time it was said to have been signed by 6 million people. A small contingent delivered the petition to Parliament, where it was rejected for a third time. It was just thirty years since Peterloo, when people had been killed and injured en masse for asking for a fair democratic system and fair wages. Since then, almost nothing had happened of much benefit to the working classes, and this latest defeat was just too much. Subsequently the Physical Force element of the Chartists came to the fore and in June of that year there were reports of widespread drilling and arming in West Yorkshire. The government rushed through the banning of public meetings and fresh legislation on sedition and treason to prevent insurrection, and transported one of the ringleaders to Australia. However, after this failure of its third and final petition, and the subsequent protests, the Chartist Movement declined. Its last National Convention was held in 1858, but demand for parliamentary reform went on.

Chapter 12

Female Suffrage

Although female suffrage had been discussed since the days of Peterloo it had not been officially made a reform demand. The Female Political Union of Newcastle, formed late in 1838, was one of the most vocal and militant women's groups, keen that females should be involved in politics and enfranchisement, constantly promoting their arguments for better wages and equal rights. Female Chartists had wanted men to be able to earn enough so that their wives and children did not have to work in the mills. Alongside their male compatriots they also campaigned for the abolition of repressive measures such as the Corn Laws, the New Poor Law, and restrictions imposed on trade union activities. Cracks were beginning to appear in the dam of male exclusivity and soon that dam would burst, and the flood gates would open. The struggle for female suffrage was about to explode.

Those women who had been at Peterloo were now ageing. Mary Fildes left the Chartist Movement in 1843 to run a pub in Chester. Susanna Inge had also resigned from the Chartist Movement in 1843, although she had continued to be vocal for the cause of female suffrage. Susannah Saxton and Alice Kitchen were approaching their sixties. Jemima Bamford was in her seventies and died in 1862.

A new generation had grown up since Peterloo however, a generation inspired by the tales of their mothers and grandmothers and determined to carry on the fight for the cause of female suffrage – but in a much more vocal and insistent manner. In 1841 William Lovett, a Cornish carpenter who believed that men and women should have equal rights, although different duties, helped to launch the National Association which, for the first time, included female suffrage on an official agenda;

while in 1840 a Salford Chartist named R.J. Richardson had written a pamphlet called 'The Rights of Women', in which he stated that,

> if a woman is qualified to be a Queen over a great nation, armed with the power of nullifying the powers of Parliament ... if it is admissible that the Queen, a woman, by the constitution of the country can command, can rule over a nation, then I say, women in every instance ought not to be excluded from her share in the executive and legislative power of the country.

It was a fine sentiment, except that the said queen herself did not agree with female suffrage.

However, a good deal of support emerged from another direction. Prior to the Industrial Revolution there had basically been the 'upper orders' and the 'lower orders' in society. A consequence of the explosion of output and trade in the world of manufacturing had been that a third 'order' had come into existence: the 'middle order' (known as the middle class today). The 'middle order', or 'middle class', owed their place in society solely to money, not to land, inheritance, rank or titles. The 'upper orders' had wealth, but they also had land, and saw themselves as 'landed gentry' of 'good breeding', who could trace their ancestors back to medieval times. In most cases there was a knighthood, baronetcy, earldom or lordship attached, which added rank and importance to wealth and 'breeding'. The 'middle orders' tended to consist of the professions, such as medicine, teaching, law, and those whose success in trade had qualified them financially to belong to this 'order'. The 'upper order' were dismissive and often referred to them contemptuously as the 'nouveau riche'. Class boundaries were strict in nineteenth century Victorian England. A serving girl could not hope to marry a doctor and a doctor could not hope to marry an upper-class girl. Those who transgressed, like the mother of the novelist D.H. Lawrence, a middle-class girl who had 'married beneath her', to a miner, were shunned and shamed by their families. The daughters of this new middle class often received a reasonable education, although they were not usually expected to go out to work; if they did, virtually the only occupations open to them were that of governess or teacher, which made them very conscious of their limitations. Charlotte Brontë famously profiled this situation in her novel *Jane Eyre*: 'Some of the best people that ever lived have been as destitute as I am; and if you are a Christian, you ought not to consider poverty a crime.' Beatrix Potter, the internationally acclaimed children's author of *Peter Rabbit*, wrote in the 1890s that she simply wanted 'to live a useful life'. Both her grandfathers were middle class and it was their money that initially enabled her to have the sort of life where she had the leisure and materials to create *Peter Rabbit*. Her paternal grandmother, Jessie Potter, the 'pretty radical' of mid-nineteenth-century Manchester, was a great influence on Beatrix. Denied an academic career in the scientific research of fungi solely on the grounds of her sex, Beatrix finally rebelled on the eve of the Great War. Using proceeds from the sales of *Peter Rabbit*, she bought a farm in the Lake District, married the solicitor who did her conveyancing, and became a well-respected breeder of Herdwick sheep. She never referred to *Peter Rabbit* again.

However, middle-class women were now branching out and choosing careers which previously had been unthinkable for females. They were very aware that further and higher education needed to be available for girls in the same manner that it was for boys. Emboldened by the way females had demonstrated at Peterloo, worked with the Chartists, formed their own unions for protection and conducted their own strikes for better wages, women like Elizabeth Garrett Anderson, Florence Nightingale, Lydia Becker, Emily Davies, Anne Knight, her friends Elizabeth Pease and Jane Smeal, now began to pioneer ways into professions hitherto completely closed to women.

Elizabeth Pease was born in Darlington, the daughter of a Quaker woollen manufacturer, twelve years before Peterloo. Her family were much involved in social reform issues, and she worked as her father's secretary, but Elizabeth, who was a close friend of Harriet Martineau, was initially mostly involved with the issues of slavery and the anti-slavery campaign. She was much influenced by the pamphlet 'Immediate Not Gradual Abolition', written by Elizabeth Heyrick, a keen social reformer and abolitionist who differed from the Anti-Slavery Society because they wanted a more gradual abolition. Most of Elizabeth Pease's fellow campaigners agreed with Elizabeth Heyrick, which annoyed William Wilberforce who headed the Anti-Slavery Society because 'for ladies to meet, to publish, to go from house to house stirring up petitions – these appear to me proceedings unsuited to the female character as delineated in Scripture.' Consequently, separate Ladies' Societies for the Relief of Negro Slaves were established and Elizabeth Pease formed a branch in Darlington. She was jubilant when the Slavery Abolition Act was passed in 1833, and she also supported the Great Reform Act of 1832, which resulted in her father, Joseph Pease, becoming the first Quaker MP. She then worked with Jane Smeal to fight for universal suffrage.

Jane Smeal was the daughter of William Smeal, a Quaker tea merchant in Glasgow; she was a leading figure in the anti-slavery movement. Jane assisted Elizabeth Pease to help women establish anti-slavery societies. Jane founded the Glasgow Ladies Emancipation Society and by 1837 there were eight such female groups. In March 1838, Jane collaborated with Elizabeth Pease to publish a pamphlet, 'Address to the Women of Great Britain', where they urged women to form female anti-slavery associations and to speak at public meetings. Later, working with Elizabeth Pease to promote the cause of female suffrage, Jane cynically remarked:

> The females in this city [Glasgow] who have much leisure for philanthropic objects are I believe very numerous – but unhappily that is not the class who take an active part in the cause here – neither the noble, the rich, nor the learned are to be found advocating our cause. Our subscribers and most efficient members are all in the middling and working classes, but they have great zeal and labour very harmoniously together.

Chelmsford-born Anne Knight came from a Quaker family who were active in the anti-slavery movement. She became fluent in French and German through her travels on the Continent, and was in her early thirties by the time of Peterloo. She was a member of Chelmsford Ladies Anti-Slavery Society by 1825, but was outraged when women were prevented from attending the World Anti-Slavery Convention in 1840. Anne Knight and her friends, Elizabeth Pease and Jane Smeal, were both Quakers and Chartists, and had been deeply involved in the anti-slavery campaign. Elizabeth Pease wrote to a friend,

> the grand principle of the natural equality of man, a principle alas almost buried in the land beneath the rubbish of an hereditary aristocracy and the force of a State religion. Working people are driven almost to desperation by those who consider they are but chattels made to minister to their luxury and add to their wealth.

In 1847, Anne Knight wrote what is believed to be one of the first leaflets on women's suffrage, but she worried 'that the class struggle took precedence over that for women's rights', and believed that 'true universal suffrage' should be campaigned for by Chartists; in 1851, she founded the Sheffield Female Political Association with Anne Kent to fight for the same cause.

Lydia Becker was born on the same street down which the cavalry had charged at Peterloo. She was a self-taught scientist who studied botany and astronomy and worked for Charles Darwin. She also encouraged girls to try and study science. In 1867 she founded the Ladies Literary Society in Manchester, but she is best known for starting the first official female suffrage movement in that same year in Manchester and for her work supporting female suffrage.

Emily Davies, a vicar's daughter from Gateshead, fought for the right for women to have an academic education on the same basis as men. In 1873, with the help of leading feminist and fellow suffragist, Barbara Bodichon, she founded Girton College in Cambridge. Emily was involved in the suffrage movement and wrote 'The Higher Education of Women' in 1866. She was also friendly with Liverpool-born Anne Clough, who was instrumental in the establishment of Newnham College in Cambridge and was its first principal.

Florence Nightingale was born the year after Peterloo in Florence, Tuscany, and named after the city, although she spent her childhood in England. When she decided to pursue a career as a nurse, for which she said she had a calling, her family were shocked and horrified. Quite apart from everything else of which they disapproved, the worst thing for them was that she would have to see naked men. Consequently, she had to work extremely hard to educate herself as a nurse. She is best known for her time in the Crimean war (1853–56) when she became known as the Lady of the Lamp because of her night-time visits to the wards to comfort badly injured and dying men. Her main contribution was to revolutionise nursing practices and to recognise the essential importance of sanitation and hygiene to good health.

Elizabeth Garrett Anderson, the sister of suffragist leader Millicent Garrett Fawcett, chalked up a whole list of 'firsts'. She was the first woman in Britain to qualify as a doctor and a surgeon; a co-founder of the first hospital staffed by women; the first dean of a British medical school; the first woman to be elected to a British school board; the first female mayor (of Aldeburgh) and the first female magistrate in the country. In 1872 she treated women for gynaecological problems at the New Hospital for Women and Children in London, and in 1874 she cofounded the London School for Medicine, the only teaching hospital in Britain for women, which is now the medical school of University College in London. Henry Maudsley wrote an article 'Sex and Mind in Education,' which was published that same year. In it he stated that 'education for women caused over-exertion which reduced their reproductive capacity, sometimes causing nervous and even mental disorders'. Elizabeth Garret Anderson countered sharply that 'the real danger for women was not education but boredom … fresh air and exercise were preferable to sitting by the fire with a novel'.

Chapter 13

Electoral Reform 1860–1867

It was now over forty years since Peterloo and still many of the working class were denied any real vote. In 1860, Lord John Russell suggested reducing the financial and property qualifications for the franchise, but even the Liberals (formerly the Whigs) were opposed to this idea, claiming it would not help to 'hand the vote to great masses of half-educated men'. In fact, once trade unionists had the vote 'they might actually demand the reduction of the working day to eight hours'. Benjamin Disraeli, a Conservative MP, was even more against it because he felt that enfranchising another 203,000 voters from the boroughs would 'encourage them to cast their votes all of one class bound together by the same entitlement and habits ... we would be conferring power on a class'. The prime minister, Lord Palmerston, was more direct. He thought the proposal was causing,

> excitement in the working class and would give great power to the agitating but secret leaders of the unions ... the direct consequence would be an increased and plausible cry for the ballot and the introduction of men into the House of Commons who would be following impulses not congenial to our institutions ... this intended course is openly disapproved of by all the intelligent and respectable classes.

In early June 1862, Disraeli made a further speech in the House of Commons designed, it would seem, to support Palmerston's views further,

> ... to build up a community, not upon Liberal opinions, which any man may fashion to his fancy, but upon popular

principles, which assert equal rights, civil and religious; to uphold the institutions of the country because they are the embodiment of the wants and wishes of the nation, and protect us alike from individual tyranny and popular outrage; equally to resist democracy and oligarchy; and favour that principle of free aristocracy which is the only basis and security for constitutional government; to be vigilant to guard and prompt to vindicate the honour of the country, but to hold aloof from that turbulent diplomacy which only distracts the mind of a people from internal improvement; to lighten taxation; frugally but wisely to administer the public treasure; to favour popular education, because it is the best guarantee for public order; to defend local government; and to be as jealous of the rights of the working man as of the prerogatives of the Crown and the privileges of the Senate—these were once the principles which regulated Tory statesmen, and I for one have no wish that the Tory party should ever be in power unless they practise them.

William Ewart Gladstone, who was then Chancellor of the Exchequer, took a different view. Although originally opposed to parliamentary reform he had changed his mind after visiting the cotton manufacturing districts and had been 'favourably impressed by working-class qualities'. The working classes were neither ignorant nor illiterate. Everyone who worked in the mills and manufactories had to be able to read instructions and warning notices. Therefore, they had to be literate. Writing was seen as a different matter and not everyone could write, but they could read. Before Charles Dickens spoke of the 'great free school bent on carrying instruction to the poorest hearths', at the opening of the first free British municipal library at Manchester in 1852, there were numerous small circulating libraries and plenty of cheap pamphlets and newspapers which workers could read to inform and educate themselves. Gladstone believed that they would exercise their right to vote in a responsible manner and in this he was supported by John Bright, who led the case for the repeal of the Corn Laws. In May 1864 he argued that only 10 per cent of those entitled to vote were 'working men'; he felt that everyone should be morally entitled to vote and that 'hearts should be bound together by a reasonable extension, at fitting times and among selected portions of the people, of every benefit and every privilege that can be justly conferred upon them'.

Lord Palmerston professed himself greatly upset by this view and demanded an apology. Gladstone was bewildered:

> I have never exhorted the working men to agitate for the franchise, and I am at a loss to conceive what report of my speech can have been construed by you in such a sense. I argued as strongly as I could against the withdrawal of the Reform Bill in 1860. I think the party which supports your Government has suffered and is suffering and will much more seriously suffer from the part which as a party it has played within these recent years, in regard to the franchise.

By 1865 the International Working Mens' Association and trade unionists were calling for 'one man one vote', and were supported by several well-known figures like John Bright, Peter Taylor, Titus Salt and John Stuart Mill. Palmerston died in the July of that year and Earl Russell became prime minister. In 1866 Gladstone took the opportunity to introduce a Bill with much reduced qualifications for the franchise which would then include many of the working classes. There were vociferous objections,

> is it not certain that in a few years from this the working men will be in a majority? Is it not certain that causes are at work which will have a tendency to multiply the franchise – that the £6 houses will become £7 ones, and that £9 houses will expand to larger ... we shall see the working classes in majority in the constituencies. Look at what that implies ... If you want

venality, if you want ignorance, if you want drunkenness, and facility for being intimidated; or if, on the other hand, you want impulsive, unreflecting, and violent people, where do you look for them in the constituencies? We know what those people are [like] who live in small houses ... The first stage, I have no doubt will be an increase of corruption, intimidation, and disorder ... The second will be that the working men of England, finding themselves in a full majority of the whole constituency, will awake to a full sense of their power.

Robert Lowe MP, 1865

The Conservatives were totally opposed to an extended franchise and Earl Russell's government, unable to get the Bill through the Commons, resigned. Consequently, the Reform League organised a street march and public meeting of 30,000 people supporting the demand for 'household suffrage'.

By now the cause of female suffrage was also growing rapidly. John Stuart Mill remained a passionate believer in a just society. He was the MP for Westminster and the first MP to call for women's suffrage in 1866. A leading advocate of female suffrage, he wanted to replace the term 'man' with that of 'person', to include women, in the Reform Bill. However, the time was not yet right and the amendment was defeated. 'We talk of political revolutions,' he said,

but we do not sufficiently attend to the fact that there has taken place around us a silent domestic revolution: women and men are, for the first time in history, really each other's companions ... when men and women are really companions, if women are frivolous men will be frivolous ... the two sexes must rise or sink together.

In 1851 Mill married Harriet Taylor, whom he had met in 1831 and with whom he shared a close relationship, as well as many ideas and principles. Harriet was born in London twelve years before Peterloo and was a great influence on her second husband, the philosopher John Stuart Mill. His father had been secretary to Jeremy Bentham, an English philosopher and social reformer. In 1818, Bentham had advocated female suffrage in his book *A Plan for Parliamentary Reform*. Harriet, a Unitarian, received a good education and was fond of writing poetry. A staunch advocate of women's rights, she criticised the unequal treatment of women and wrote about a number of women's issues including several articles on female inequality and domestic violence. Harriet had liked Mill from the moment she met him because 'he treated her like an equal'. In 1833 they collaborated on a series of essays entitled simply *On Marriage*. The essays discussed the questions of marriage, separation and divorce. Harriet insisted that was what was necessary

> to rais[e] the condition of women was 'to remove all interference with affection, or with anything which is, or which even might be supposed to be, demonstrative of affection.' She felt it was wrong that 'women are educated for one single object, to gain their living by marrying'; and that 'to be married is the object of their existence ... that object being gained they do really cease to exist as to anything worth calling life or any useful purpose.'

She criticised the unfair hypocrisy that any girl seen as

> 'suitable for marriage is – because only virgins are seen as suitable – by that very fact completely ignorant as to what marriage entails.' She also argued for the right to divorce, saying 'who would wish to have the person without the inclination?' Harriet added 'certain it is that there is equality in nothing now – all the pleasure ... being men's, and all the disagreeables and pains being women's', it is equally certain that 'pleasure would be infinitely heightened both in kind and

degree by the perfect equality of the sexes ... sex in its true
and finest meaning, seems to be the way in which is manifested
all that is highest, best and beautiful in the nature of human
beings – none but poets have approached to the perception of
the beauty of the material world – still less of the spiritual –
and there never yet existed a poet except by the inspiration of
that feeling which is the perception of beauty in all forms and
by all means which are given us.

When they married in 1851, Harriet continued to collaborate with
her husband and in that same year they wrote a long essay on *The
Enfranchisement of Women*. In it they stated unequivocally,

that women have as good a claim as men have ... to the
suffrage, or to a place in the jury box ... but this is for one
sex only ... 'life, liberty, and the pursuit of happiness' are
'inalienable rights ... the contradiction between principle and
practice cannot be explained away. A like dereliction of the
fundamental maxims of political creed has been committed
by the Americans in the flagrant instance of the negroes'.
They continued by calling out 'Radicals and Chartists in
the British Islands, and democrats on the Continent, who
claim what is called universal suffrage as an inherent right, is
unjustly and oppressively withheld from them. For with what
truth or rationality could the suffrage be termed universal,
while half the human species remain excluded from it? The
Chartist who denies the suffrage to women is a Chartist only
because he is not a lord. Even those who do not look upon
a voice in the government as a matter of personal right, nor
profess principles which require that it should be extended
to all, have usually traditional maxims of political justice
with which it is impossible to reconcile the exclusion of all
women from the common rights of citizenship. It is an axiom

of English freedom, that taxation and representation should be co-extensive. Even under the laws which give the wife's property to the husband, there are many unmarried women who pay taxes. It is one of the fundamental doctrines of the British Constitution, that all persons should be tried by their peers; yet women, whenever tried, are tried by male judges and a male jury. To foreigners, the law accords the privilege of claiming that half the jury should be composed of themselves: not so to women. In all things, the presumption ought to be on the side of equality. A reason must be given why anything should be permitted to one person, and interdicted to another ... even in the exercise of industry, almost all employments which task the higher faculties in an important field, which lead to distinction, riches, or even pecuniary independence, are fenced round as the exclusive domain of the predominant section, scarcely any doors being left open to the dependent class ... we are firmly convinced that the division of mankind into two castes, one born to rule over the other is in this case, as in all cases, is an unqualified mischief'.

Harriet Taylor Mill also read and commented on all her husband's work and he found her a great inspiration. He was devastated when she died aged only 51 in 1858. In 1869, eleven years after her death, he wrote his famous essay on 'The Subjection of Women': 'the whole of the female sex were simply slaves ... the legal subordination of one sex to the other − [which] is wrong itself, and now one of the chief hindrances to human improvement; and it ought to be replaced by a principle of perfect equality,' and three major issues which hindered equality for women were 'society and gender construction, education and marriage' and that 'the oppression of women was one of the few remaining relics from ancient times, a set of prejudices that severely impeded the progress of humanity.' He also condemned the notion of slavery, to which many nineteenth century women were subject even though technically they were not slaves.

> This absolutely extreme case of the law of force, condemned by those who can tolerate almost every other form of arbitrary power, and which, of all others, presents features the most revolting to the feeling of all who look at it from an impartial position, was the law of civilized and Christian England within the memory of persons now living: and in one half of Anglo-Saxon America three or four years ago, not only did slavery exist, but the slave trade, and the breeding of slaves expressly for it, was a general practice between slave states. Yet not only was there a greater strength of sentiment against it, but, in England at least, a less amount either of feeling or of interest in favour of it, than of any other of the customary abuses of force: for its motive was the love of gain, unmixed and undisguised: and those who profited by it were a very small numerical fraction of the country, while the natural feeling of all who were not personally interested in it, was unmitigated abhorrence.

The essay was a fitting tribute to Harriet.

Chapter 14

The Second Reform Act 1867

William Gladstone had evolved from Conservative to Liberal Party and became leader of the Liberals in 1867. As Chancellor he had revoked the paper tax and reduced income tax and he had been lauded by the working classes for doing so. In 1865 George Holyoak wrote,

> When Mr Gladstone visited the North, you well remember when word passed from the newspaper to the workman that it circulated through mines and mills, factories and workshops, and they came out to greet the only British minister who ever gave the English people a right because it was just they should have it ... and when he went down the Tyne, all the country heard how twenty miles of banks were lined with people who came to greet him. Men stood in the blaze of chimneys; the roofs of factories were crowded; colliers came up from the mines; women held up their children on the banks that it might be said in after life that they had seen the Chancellor of the People go by. The river was covered like the land. Every man who could ply an oar pulled up to give Mr Gladstone a cheer ... the people were grateful to him, and rough pitmen who never approached a public man before, pressed round his carriage by thousands ... and thousands of arms were stretched out at once, to shake hands with Mr Gladstone as one of themselves.

Lord Palmerston had been against giving further voting concessions to the working classes. However, subsequently, Benjamin Disraeli had realised that continued Conservative opposition to reform would reflect badly on the Conservative Party and increase radicalism, which would only serve to strengthen Gladstone's stance that they should have it. Disraeli introduced his new Reform Act in March 1867, but it had been moderated to give fewer working-class males the vote and to increase the number of votes for graduates and professionals. For some people, this was not enough. Robert Cecil resigned in protest against this proposed extension of democracy. However, as Disraeli explained to him, it had little to do with democracy: 'We do not live – and I trust it will never be the fate of this country to live – under a democracy.' The Reform League staged another demonstration, this time with 50,000 people in Hyde Park. It was peaceful and although troops were on standby, they were not used. Memories of Peterloo were still too recent. There were demands for the organisers to be arrested but Disraeli resisted, not wanting to cause more civil unrest. Instead he modified the adaptation of his Reform Bill, much to the disgust of the vociferous Robert Lowe: 'Wiltshire labourers earning eight shillings a week … what will their politics be? With every disposition to speak favourably of them, their politics must take one form or another of socialism and with this reform we are going to make a revolution.'

Nevertheless change was continuing. About 1,500,000 males (every male adult borough householder) got the vote, and the cities of Liverpool, Manchester, Birmingham and Leeds got an extra seat, as did fifteen towns which had never had a seat, and some counties whose populations had grown larger. The dual vote, allowing people with properties in both town and country to vote twice, was abolished, and the requirement for two-years residence for ratepayers was reduced to one year. It was progress but progress was slow.

Chapter 15

The Third Reform Act 1884

In 1884, the 65th anniversary of Peterloo, the Third Reform Act which would extend the vote to agricultural workers went before the Commons but was rejected by the Lords until a Redistribution Bill had been passed. This would allow 50,000 voters per each single member constituency. It was progress, but 40 per cent of males and 100 per cent of females remained disenfranchised. It was too much for those who felt they had spent most of their lives waiting for democratic justice and too much for younger females who were growing impatient. A number of Reform demonstrations were held, especially in the Manchester area which had suffered so badly from the tragedy of Peterloo, notably one which took place in Failsworth near Oldham. On 25 September the *Oldham Evening Chronicle* published preparations for the procession to mark the 65th anniversary of Peterloo. Eleven Peterloo veterans who lived locally were invited to attend, and it was arranged that they would carry Sam Bamford's tattered banner which Bamford had carried himself at Peterloo. The *Oldham Chronicle* covered the event in detail.

'The Great Reform Demonstration', a gathering of major importance, took place on Saturday, 27 September 1884. It was a protest against the blocking of a new Franchise Bill by the House of Lords. Failsworth in Lancashire was strongly Liberal in its politics and local elections were taking place in the area at the same time.

'Since the 1832 Reform Bill, Failsworth has become "a political centre" in "regards to the numbers of Liberals" but the Franchise Bill was blocked in its present form and would deprive Failsworth of some political rights [if amended as per the House of Lords wishes] and therefore the demonstration was in favour of extending the franchise.'

Surprisingly, for the times, there were as many women as men involved in the demand for reform although female suffrage was not yet on the official agenda.

'The day was perfect. The sun shone, there were blue skies and a light breeze, just like the day of Peterloo', but it was 'a calm reasonable day' in contrast to Peterloo. The comparison was not lost on the veterans. Newton, Woodhouses, Oldham Radical Association (whose banner stated 'Liberty, Equality, Fraternity'), Hollinwood and the Free Liberal Club sent contingents. There were a number of banners in the procession as well as Sam Bamford's Peterloo banner, and slogans included:

'House of Lords ... ended or mended'
'People's Bill, People's Will'
'Down with the House of Lords'
'The People's House shall prevail'
'For freedom and justice we plead'

Lots of folk wore hats adorned with portraits of politicians – 'Gladstone's portrait proliferated'. Different professions marched in groups. The bakers brought a Franchise loaf weighing about 40lbs, a 'Gladstone loaf' weighing about 10lb, and a small spare Tory loaf of no consequence to represent the two million unenfranchised folk who had no vote, Gladstone's efforts at extending the franchise, and the numbers of Tories who were in a minority, but held all the power. The loaves were followed by 'a donkey dressed in blue and labelled "a born Lord"'.

The Representation of the People Act 1884 (known as the Third Reform Act) extended suffrage rights further from the Reform Act of 1867. This meant that the same voting qualifications which existed in the towns now existed in the countryside and the 'one member constituency would become the normal pattern for Parliamentary representation'. At this time the electorate was just over 5.5 million. However, the House of Lords, led by Lord Salisbury, took great exception to this legislation and blocked it, claiming that such an Act could not possibly be passed until a Redistribution of Seats Act had been passed. In Failsworth this provoked great anger since only 137 of the 8,000 population could vote in the first place. 'How can you distribute seats for just 137 voters?' one old lady asked in bewildered irritation. The eleven veterans who were in St Peter's Field on that summer day sixty-five years before must have wondered what it had all been for: the sacrifices and the suffering. There had been changes, but not enough. There were still large numbers of disenfranchised folk, female suffrage was not even on the horizon and, for most people, this action by the House of Lords was a step too far, causing great resentment.

The audience was a large one, including the Lancashire writer Ben Brierley and the Peterloo veterans, watching the procession of protest and listening to the speakers afterwards. There were a number of speakers, including Robert Leake, MP for South Manchester, and William Trevor, a local political journalist, and two platforms. Robert Leake gave an opening speech thanking Gladstone for his franchise efforts, but condemning the House of Lords for their opposition.

Number one platform attracted an audience of over 2,000. William Trevor proposed the first motion, thanking Gladstone for understanding the true meaning of freedom and wishing the Franchise Bill all success to enfranchise another 2 million citizens. After the Bill had been rejected, it was claimed that Lord Salisbury had invented reasons for rejection. The Lords wanted redistribution coupled with the Franchise Bill, but how did one redistribute just 137 votes. He felt 'the maxim [of] taxation without representation had been regarded as unjust for centuries'.

The Irish Party, following the advice of Charles Stewart Parnell, had also voted against the Bill. Parnell was keen to obtain a resolution of the Irish question on Home Rule by supporting Conservative policies. Luke Pollitt of Newton Heath said that 'the Liberal government was paving the way for man's franchise through education'.

Richard Leake MP stated that the Liberal Party 'had a broad, inclusive yet simple proposition on the Franchise question'. Mr A.E. Reyner JP, of Ashton, proposed the second motion, amid calls for 'reform of the irresponsible and hereditary House', that 'the Bill had to be presented again and Gladstone had to advise Her Majesty, Queen Victoria, to overcome the obstructions in the House of Lords'. He took the view that the queen was sensible and would accept advice. Folk understood that a Redistribution Bill 'would follow on naturally', because that would be 'fair, upright and honourable', but the Lords were currently insisting that they must be passed together.

There was a great deal of discussion of the injustice of the stance taken by the House of Lords and a lot of anger against Lord Salisbury, who had spearheaded the rejection campaign and, said W.H. Holland, 'had then gone on holiday to his villa in the South of France'.

The second platform was addressed by Joe Thomas, an unenfranchised householder, who proposed the first motion stating that 'if the Lords rejected the motion again they should be abolished!' He continued, 'the Tory motto was to do nothing' resulting in an attitude of 'up with the Peers and down with the People'. This resolution was seconded by Councillor Emmett who praised 'the unanimity and enthusiasm of the demonstration'.

John Slagg MP stated 'we were in front of a crisis which was of the most serious moment', adding that the 'nobility were blocking the peasants' because votes equated with power, so 'a man without a vote was a political cypher'. The resolution was carried amid much cheering. Charles Shaw proposed the second resolution. He stated that 'If the Tory Party was governed by the rashness of Lord Salisbury, the issue of abolition would be ultimately forced.' He went on, 'The House of Lords had no right to say that the House of Commons did not represent the people.' He wondered if 'the House of Lords were in league with the Tories to resist progressive measures … if the House of Lords could not submit or accept what was reasonable then they should be abolished.'

Mr Pollitt of Newton Heath seconded the resolution, supported by Mr Leake MP who was received with much enthusiasm. Mr Leake believed it was a revolutionary resolution but 'as a responsible MP and legislator he could not disagree with its terms'. The resolution was passed unanimously.

Although unable to attend due to House of Commons work, Mr Agnew MP supported the demonstration in a letter. He thought 'the Lords' actions reprehensible in rejecting the Bill and threatening the House of Commons' and he hoped that 'the whole matter will be fairly and civilly resolved'.

There were many similar demonstrations but this one is particularly well recorded, especially as the son of one of the veterans was a writer and was friendly with a local journalist.

Chapter 16

Peterloo Veterans 1884 ... and Who was Mary Collins?

Consequently, two months later, on 29 November, the *Oldham Weekly Chronicle* published 'A Night with the Peterloo Veterans', based on their memories as they had sat and talked over tea after the demonstration.

> 'One class of people whose company I enjoy,' the journalist wrote, 'is old and sturdy reformers who in ... bygone days ... have played in the noble struggle for the charter of human rights and liberty ...

> The present reform agitation suggested to a friend of mine the idea of entertaining at tea all the Peterloo veterans now living in the area of Failsworth ... and by special invitation I was present at the interesting gathering.

> There were eleven of these old veteran performers. They were mostly residents of Failsworth and their age average is nearly 82 ... and a prominent MP was a special guest. Seven were men and four were women. As I sat and gazed ... and listened I could not help but feel moved. The tears of gratitude flowed as I thought of the liberties we now enjoy and how they had been fought for ... by these political heroes ... the reminiscences ... will perhaps be of interest.'

There was hearty singing of Henry Hunt and Liberty:

> O, God bless Hunt and Wellesley
> With them we'll take a part;
> To gain our rights and liberty
> We'll join both hands and heart

The journalist had paused here for a few moments and then continued:

> Addressing the singer ... I asked ... if he had a good recollection of Peterloo events. 'Remember it!' and so he should ... he nearly got killed that day. When the Yeomanry rushed upon them he made his escape and took refuge in a cellar where a lot of his fellow reformers followed. In the bustle he was thrown down and trampled on and badly hurt. It was with great difficulty that he got home ... there were many horrible things done that day never appeared in the newspapers ... there were more butchers together that day ... nor he had seen since. A few of the Yeomanry were from that district but they were ever after ashamed ... The regular soldiers behaved themselves ... in comparison to the Yeomanry ... if it had not been for them there would have been more killed. It were [*sic*] a barbarous thing.

> Here the old man burst out singing a song descriptive of the massacres. The song finished, another veteran ... narrated his experience. He lost his hat and a shoe in the struggle ... he was glad to get away as well. Coming home through Newton Heath ... he met a man carrying a bundle of shoes and hats ... he had picked up after the field had been cleared, and he was supplying all he met who had lost such things. The narrator said he tried shoes and hats until he was fitted and, on leaving the shoes and hats distributor, he was told ... to tell all who had

lost such head and foot gear that they might have any ... that would fit them. That kind-hearted soul came from Copster Hill, Oldham.

The question was asked were there a great many at Peterloo from Failsworth. An old man replied ... 'Amongst the Failsworth contingent there were twenty-four young women dressed in white garments' with ... deep emotion he was sorry to say 'that some of the fair damsels were hurt in the struggle'. One of the young women, Mrs Dunkerley, had the stave cut out of her hands three times by the Yeomanry. Each time she picked up the banner and cried 'Hunt and Liberty forever!'

Some of those wild mad Yeomanry were drunk upon their horses ... they met in St James' Square and were made drunken there before they could do their dirty work ... he had watched the Tories from 1816 and could remember ... they kept grain in a store in Liverpool until it was spoiled and people were nearly starved to death at the time. This was done to get up the price of grain. Large quantities were spoiled and had to be destroyed. Flour was up to 6s a dozen ... he remembered fetching six penny-worth in a basin. Wages were low ... and provisions high ... the press being gagged it was difficult to get any redress. They would not let the nation become wealthy when it might have done. Everything you touched ... was taxed ... soap was taxed ... the looking glass was taxed ... you put a clean collar on, the starch that stiffened it was taxed ... they used to fetch thin starch ... from a house where it was retailed out in a custard form at so much a lump ... On being asked how they spent their leisure time he could hardly tell ... fourteen of them one Christmas Day arranging to join at making treacle toffy [sic] but they found ... that they had not sufficient to purchase a pound of treacle, the price being so high. These were 'the good old times' the Tories were fond of talking about.

An old dame of 83 [Mary Collins] promised to sing a song if someone would keep her pipe in ... as the singer was finishing her song ... fifteen verses ... she observed that the person who had promised to keep her pipe in had become so fascinated ... he had failed in his promise. A recitation was given next by ... a dame of 88 [Catherine McMurdo] ... a remarkable feat of memory.

Afterwards it was asked if any of them had ever suffered imprisonment for their opinions. 'Aye!' replied a veteran Radical. 'I was put in ... shaved, powd [hair cut] and robbed.' Another ... said he had a brother arrested and tried for a capital offence ... but his brother proved that he had been in Quebec at the time of the offence. These were hard times ... you could hardly tell who were friends and who were foes and spies. Spies had pikes and arms and hid things ... then went with law officials and found what they had secreted ... spies would have sworn anyone's life away for ... 'blood money'. The press had been gagged and durst not speak out. The old lady singer [said] 'she could remember going up White Moss before four o'clock one morning to drill. They had sticks instead of guns. This was only done to frighten Parliament. They never intended to fight.'

She should never forget the scene at Peterloo that day. Henry Hunt had urged them, before going to Peterloo, to take nothing with them, not even sticks ... He wanted a peaceful meeting but they never gave them the chance to get away. The drunken Yeomanry came rushing upon them without even waiting until the Riot Act was read as they meant to take Hunt with them ...

it was both cruel and barbarous … the regular soldiers behaved themselves like gentlemen compared with the Yeomanry … she believed the attack was arranged days before …

We were informed by another old man that four of his brothers were … at Peterloo … his father … went to meet his sons … on his way he met several Reformers … their faces sprinkled with blood and one man had a tall silk hat cut in two … one poor fellow coming through Failsworth bleeding heavily from wounds he had received … and three or four Tories … he knew … laughed in [his] face … and told him it served him right … party politics were stronger than human sympathy … None of his brothers were hurt. The old man also … remembered, shortly after the Peterloo massacre, a Radical Reformer … name of Billy Quick … near Quick's house in the old road near Wrigley Head, Failsworth … talking about reform when Billy saw mounted soldiers approaching … he darted quickly down the valley towards Moston … By twisting and turning he got clear away and was never captured … Quick by name and quick by nature. What had Quick done? Nothing. His crime was daring to be a Radical.

Such are a few of the … incidents related by the Reformers of 1819. What a … change has taken place since … Many of the reforms advocated … have now been secured. 'They laboured, and we are enjoying … the fruits of their labours.' We honour and bless them for having fearlessly done their duty, and for having been persecuted for righteousness's sake.

Oldham Chronicle, November 1884

Frustratingly, the paper did not allude to names of the speakers; although it was possible to identify the females, who were fewer in number, by their ages. Ages were not given for any of the male speakers.

It was an historic occasion, for within ten years most of the veterans were dead (two of them in the late autumn shortly after the reform demonstration) and living memory of Peterloo had passed into history. There is a photograph taken of these eleven people in 1884. To date it is the only known group photographic image of those who were at Peterloo and included:

- Chadderton, Thomas, born in Failsworth 1802, died in Pendleton 4 December 1884
- Collins, Mary, of Irish extraction, born 1801, date and place of death unknown
- Davies, John, silk weaver, born 1807, died 1888 in Failsworth
- Dawson, Jonathan, cotton weaver, born 1803, died 1891 in Failsworth
- Hilton, David, handloom silk weaver, born 1806, died near Prestwich in 1890
- McMurdo, Catherine, born 1797/1798 in Failsworth, died in Prestwich 1888
- Ogden, Thomas, handloom silk weaver, born 1804, died 1891 in Failsworth
- Schofield, Alice, daughter of radical Peter Fletcher, born 1805, died 3 November 1884 in Failsworth
- Schofield, Thomas, father of writer Sim Schofield, born 1803, died 1887 in Failsworth
- Water, Richard, cotton weaver, born 1814 (so only a child at Peterloo), died in Oldham late 1880s
- Whittaker, Susannah, weaver, born 1804, died 1890 in Failsworth

Ten of the eleven clearly lived locally, in or near Failworth, for most of their lives and are traceable through the census returns, but Mary Collins presents an enduring mystery. It is not possible to ascertain if

Collins is her married or maiden name. Although she must have lived in, or stayed near, Failsworth in 1819, because she drilled for the march up on White Moss, there is no record of her in the local census returns of that time. There is no record of her either in the later census returns for the area. She may have moved, but kept in touch with her former comrades. It is possible her name was misspelt, although this might be considered unlikely as she spent a whole evening in the company of the journalist who wrote the article and whose father was one of the eleven veterans. The only Mary Collins listed in the Manchester area census returns for 1881, who was born in Ireland in 1801, lived on Cleaver Street in Blackburn where she was a lodger and a domestic servant. She was also listed on the 1861 census at the same address with the same occupation. Blackburn is 26½ miles from Failsworth, where the 1884 demonstration took place. There was a smallpox epidemic in Blackburn in 1886 and possibly she died during that epidemic. A few early individual photographs exist from the 1860s of around half a dozen people who were also at Peterloo and include Samuel Collins (who had a sister named Mary, but she had died in 1875), William Rowbottom, Samuel Bamford, Jemima Bamford, and Mary Fildes. Ordinary people caught up in extraordinary events. They had lived long enough to see reforms in education, working conditions and social problems, as well as a number of rights for women being introduced and voting eligibility extended to many males in the wake of Peterloo, but women were still fighting hard for any kind of female suffrage.

Electoral Reform 1884

William Gladstone had managed to extend the vote to agricultural labourers with the 1884 Reform Act (which gave counties the same franchise as boroughs), adult male householders and £10 (£1,220 today) lodgers, adding 6 million to the number of people who could vote in parliamentary elections. Inevitably, the Redistribution of Seats Act had followed in 1885, but there was no mention of female suffrage. Nevertheless, even Gladstone was becoming uneasy about the direction in which British politics was moving. Writing to Lord Acton in February 1885, Gladstone criticised 'Tory democracy as "demagogism" that puts down pacific, law-respecting, economic elements that ennobled the old Conservatives but still, in secret, as obstinately attached as ever to the evil principle of class interests'. He wrote that,

> contemporary Liberalism is better, but far from being good … this Liberalism's 'pet idea' is what they call construction, that is to say, taking into the hands of the state the business of the individual man … Both Tory Democracy and this new Liberalism have done much to estrange me, and have done so for many, many years.

However, universal suffrage would not come for another thirty-four years after the Great Reform Demonstration and twenty-four years after Gladstone's death.

Chapter 17

Employment and Working Conditions for Women and Children After Peterloo

Rural life on farms or in villages had been depressed in the late eighteenth century so, encouraged by stories of good wages and better living conditions in the city, country people had migrated to Manchester in their thousands, hoping for the chance of a better life. Cotton-mill owners had been delighted. The reality, of course, was rather different. There was great competition for jobs so that it was an employers' market, useful for holding down wages. Cotton-mill life was very different and regimented by the clock. Queues of people wanting work formed outside the factory gates by 6 am every morning. Those who were not punctual could find the gates were closed by 6.01 am. It came as a great shock to country-folk mentality, for the cows had never minded whether they were milked at 6 am, 6.15 am or 6.30 am, as long as they got milked, and it is said that this absolute adherence to the very minute was responsible for the British obsession with the clock and punctuality. The mills have long gone, but the mindset has not. For once, women had the advantage in that their fingers were smaller and nimbler than those of men, so were often better suited to the spinning and weaving procedures, and they could be paid less than men. Better still, they could bring their children with them and they would work for even less wages, but every penny was welcome. It cost money to shut down cotton manufacturing machinery for cleaning, and children were small enough to be able to crawl underneath the machinery while it was still moving to clean and de-fluff the moving parts. Health and safety was totally ignored and, of course, there were numerous accidents. Workers lost limbs and children lost scalps, but many employers considered workers and their children to be totally expendable. There were always more to fill the vacancies.

Friedrich Engels described what it was like living and working in the city in his book *The Condition of the Working Class in England*. Central Manchester was 'a place of filth, ruin and uninhabitableness … it was … hell upon earth'. A pall of smoke and smog hung constantly over the city so that the sun was only seen as a dim red disc giving little light. Health and Safety regulations did not exist. The noise in the mills was such that sign language had to be used between operatives. The noise of a working mill, like Quarry Bank Mill near Manchester Airport, is so loud that today no one is allowed more than ten minutes exposure. In the Irish community off Oxford Road, there were 'women made unfit for childbearing, children deformed, men enfeebled, limbs crushed, whole generations wrecked, afflicted with disease and infirmity, purely to fill the pockets of bourgeoisie' (Friedrich Engels 1842–1844). The first Medical Officer of Health was not appointed in Manchester until 1868; this was not done out of a philanthropic concern for the working classes however, but rather the realisation that infectious diseases did not recognise class barriers and that the children of the upper classes were also at risk. One in five Manchester men was condemned as unfit when enlisting for the Boer War (1899–1902).

In 1810, Robert Owen, a philanthropic Welsh born textile manufacturer, had made himself unpopular in manufacturing quarters by campaigning for an eight-hour day with the slogan 'Eight hours labour. Eight hours recreation. Eight hours sleep.' He was also an advocate of workers' rights, laws protecting child labour and free education for children. His efforts finally resulted in the 1819 Cotton Mills and Factories Act/Twelve Hours Act (first introduced by Sir Robert Peel in 1815) being passed, forbidding employment of children under 9, limiting work to twelve hours for children aged 9-16 years, and forbidding night-work for all children. This was largely ignored by many mill owners. Child labour was cheap and useful. Many child workers were present at Peterloo and, like their parents, would try to hide the fact if they had been hurt during the massacre for fear that their employers would throw them out on to the streets. The Twelve Hours Act, however, was as far as the Conservative government of the day was prepared to go; but after the Whigs (Liberals) came to power in 1830, this initial Factory Act was followed by the 1833 Factory Act, which reiterated that no children under 9 could work in factories (except in silk mills); children under 13 were to work no more than nine hours per day and forty-eight hours per week; under 18s not to work nights; paid inspectors appointed; two eight-hour shifts a day allowed for children. This Act was also much ignored by mill owners, but many parents colluded because they simply couldn't afford to feed their children. The 1833 Act was an attempt to try and improve the lot of working children in the post-Peterloo depression, but for many it was simply impractical because workers' wages had remained very low.

There has been claim and counter claim about Britain's empire being built on child labour but contemporary nineteenth century written documentation exists which shows that children as young as 7 (occasionally younger) were working full time in the mills during the 1830s and early 1840s. Concern over child labour had been an issue since the early 1780s, and horror stories of the treatment of child labour abounded from the inner-city mills of townships like Ancoats and Chorlton-cum-Hardy, occasionally even from the more philanthropic institutions, such as Quarry Bank Mill, and clearly illustrate what children endured. Quarry Bank Mill, which was out in the country, housed its 'apprentices' (as child workers were euphemistically termed) in a custom-built Apprentice House. The children fared rather better than their urban counterparts, living in the country with its comparatively fresh air, receiving regular meals and an hour of education each day. However, two of the three regular meals (breakfast and lunch) consisted of solid onion flavoured lumps of porridge which the children could eat while continuing to work, and meat was often restricted to Sundays. A doctor, who happened to be the uncle of the writer Elizabeth Gaskell, visited twice a week. His treatment and prescription books survive and he expressed concern about the ages of the youngest apprentices. Common ailments were chest complaints, constipation and stomach problems. Some children suffered terrible homesickness and wanted their mothers, who might live as far away as Liverpool. Being unable to wait for the annual visit allowed, a few children ran away, but they were usually found quickly, brought back and punished. It was as hard for the mothers as for the children for them to be sent away, but the mothers thought it was the best chance for their children, and descriptions of how and where and under what conditions their children would be working were often heavily embroidered.

During this time, mothers working in the mills with their children often grieved to see what their children endured, but they were, at this point, powerless to do much about it. Ironically, it was often the male trade unionists who pushed for restrictions improving the lot of women and children, but this was as much out of a desire to preserve their own jobs and wage levels as any philanthropic concept. In 1842, an Act was passed banning women and boys from working underground in the mines. They didn't have the same physical strength as men and they were more likely to suffer from health problems. In any case there was a growing awareness in the middle and upper classes about the way the working class and their children were being treated. Profit was everything and millworkers' children were despised by many millowners. However, some sort of social conscience was beginning to emerge and, at the same time, the unions were becoming more of a vehicle for skilled workers and higher earners. These two factors combined pushed through more reform. The 1844 Factory Act, which covered textile factories, banned all children under 8 from working; children under 13 could work no more than six-and-a-half hours per day; while all women and children were to work no more than twelve hours a day. This caused an outcry from many working-class men who did not want their means of extra income reduced.

Three years later in 1847 came the Ten Hours Act, banning women and children working more than ten hours a day in textile factories, which caused howls of protest from both men and women of the working class; notwithstanding that the women had to go home from the mills and start work again in the home. The hours were long, but wages were still less than had been expected. Although the Ten Hours Act had been passed, there was nothing to stop employees agreeing voluntarily to work longer hours. In any case, if asked, what choice did they have? To add to their woes, in 1842 the first peacetime income tax had been levied at $7d$ in the pound and the hated Corn Laws, the protective duties which kept the price of bread high and which had been so controversial at the time of Peterloo, were still in force twenty-five years later. Rent took half a family's income in London, even if they all lived in one room. In Manchester some of the poorest families lived in one room in damp basements. Tucked into an 'oxbow' on the River Medlock, near the present Oxford Road railway station, was the area known as 'Little Ireland' due to the large number of Irish immigrants who lived there. Many had emigrated as a result of the Irish potato famine in the 1840s. Engels described Little Ireland as,

> about 200 cottages, built chiefly back-to-back, in which live
> about 4,000 human beings … the cottages are old, dirty, and
> of the smallest sort, the streets uneven, fallen into ruts and in
> part without drains or pavement; masses of refuse, offal, and
> sickening filth lie among standing pools in all directions.

He went on to say how 'a horde of ragged women and children swarm about here, filthy as the swine that thrive upon the garbage heaps and in the puddles'.

Overcrowding was rife. Disease was rife. Cholera, typhoid and TB were rife. In some areas, infant mortality was as high as four in ten. Anyone who could afford to do so lived as far from the mills as they could. Some had no choice. Some, desperate to escape, turned to prostitution, which they hoped would earn them enough money for a better life, only to find that 'the wages of sin' were sexually transmitted diseases, not a ticket to a better life.

Women still had no real rights, and many were beginning to despair. It wasn't that nothing was being done. Rebuilding was taking place and improvements in sanitation were gradually being made. It was that women still had no control over their lives; no power to act independently; no rights to their own money or property, and no vote. They had supported their menfolk loyally, but had reaped little of the rewards. Peterloo seemed just a tarnished, tragic memory. However, two north country girls, born within a year of each other shortly after Peterloo and who grew up among those with a strong living memory of the event, were destined to change the lives of British women forever.

Josephine Butler and Lydia Becker were two very different personalities. Lydia was an academic who had worked for Darwin and campaigned for girls to be taught science. In Manchester she had begun the first movement for female suffrage in 1868 and become a role model for Emmeline Pankhurst, winning the vote for Manx women decades before English women (see Female Suffrage). Josephine was a social reformer, educationalist and a feminist who exposed the trade of young female prostitutes (some as young as 12) from England to the Continent.

Josephine Butler was born in Northumberland and married an Oxford don. She spent some time in Liverpool with her husband, who had been appointed the headmaster of Liverpool College. Josephine was a firm supporter of female suffrage, believing that women would benefit immensely from better education and, together with another suffragist supporter, Anne Clough, she helped to establish the North of England Council for Promoting the Higher Education of Women, a cause dear to Lydia Becker's heart. She also campaigned hard for legal recognition of married women until the Married Women's Property Act was passed in 1882, and she continued to campaign for the amendments to the Contagious Diseases Act, backed by the Norfolk feminist writer,

Harriet Martineau, and by Florence Nightingale, until finally, in 1885, the 'compulsory examination of women' under the Contagious Diseases Acts was repealed. A major health problem for women was the question of sexually transmitted diseases (STDs). These were always seen as solely the fault of the female sex. Women suffering from STDs could be imprisoned and sentenced to hard labour. Men were not held accountable in any way.

The police in the late 1800s were harsh with women they suspected of having STDs. They were taken to the local police station where a male police officer would subject them to a rough, often painful manual examination of their intimate areas before forcibly inserting a cold steel speculum to examine them internally. Josephine Butler dubbed it 'steel rape', and fought hard for amendments to the Contagious Diseases Acts. Women who were subjected to these examinations might actually be clean, healthy, and totally innocent of what they were accused, but the slur remained. The fact of having undergone such an examination ruined their reputations so that no one would employ them and this actually forced some of them into prostitution to earn a living. Butler found a lot of support among working-class men who were against this practice, because working-class women were particularly harassed in this manner in Manchester, especially those from the poverty-stricken Ancoats, Angel Meadow, and Little Ireland localities.

Some of the pimps who lived off the immoral earnings of the prostitutes under their control pelted Josephine with cow dung in protest. The bias of the legislation against women was generally explained by stating that 'there is no comparison to be made between prostitutes and the men who consort with them … with the one sex the offence is committed as a matter of gain; with the other it is an irregular indulgence of a natural impulse.' Any woman whom a man considered to be poorly dressed or talking inappropriately could be deemed a whore. Any woman living with a man to whom she was not married was considered a prostitute. In fact, any female who did not conform to the strict conventional attitudes was considered 'loose, unsuitable, unpleasant, and probably a whore'. Victorian attitudes were slow to subside and persisted until at least the 1960s.

In the same year of 1885 that the Contagious Diseases Act was repealed, Josephine Butler had met Florence Soper Booth, the daughter-in-law of William Booth, founder of the Salvation Army, and was horrified to learn the extent of child prostitution in Britain. Plenty of young girls were sold into prostitution in London from the inner-city millscape slums of Manchester by parents and relatives desperate to make up the household incomes to a sufficient level to pay the rent and put food on the table. Many were either told, or told themselves, that the girls would be looked after and cared for properly and would have a better life than working for slave wages in the dangerous environment of the mills. This, of course, was far from the truth, and countless young lives were ruined, but the Victorian double standards of 'boys will be boys', who sometimes needed 'an irregular indulgence of a natural impulse' (although they expected their own daughters to 'be pure and chaste'), legitimised the use of young girls in this way. Besides, to Victorian class-ridden culture, they were only the daughters of the very lowest classes and, as such, didn't merit any care or consideration.

In any case it was quite simple to deny that such practices existed. The word of these girls would count for nothing against the word of 'upright, decent, moral' Victorian males. There were, however, a considerable number of men who did not find such practices acceptable and one of them was William Stead, editor of the *Pall Mall Gazette*. His problem was that he knew young girls were also being purchased in many other large towns and cities for prostitution, but proving it was quite another problem. Therefore, he hatched a plan with Josephine and Florence. He made contacts through their work with hostels for destitute women and former prostitutes, and he purchased a 13-year-old girl in a Marylebone slum for whom he paid £5 (around £250 today) to her mother. He took her to France and then he began a series of articles under the heading 'The Maiden Tribute of Modern Babylon'.

In the first one he reproduced part of an interview he had with Howard Vincent, the head of CID in London.

Stead: 'But do you mean to tell me that in very truth actual rapes, in the legal sense of the word, are constantly being perpetrated in London on unwilling virgins, purveyed and procured to rich men at so much a head by keepers of brothels?'

Vincent: 'Certainly. There is not a doubt of it.'

Stead: 'Why the very thought is enough to raise hell.'

Vincent: 'It is true, and although it ought to raise hell, it does not even raise the neighbours.'

Victorian Britain was finally shocked out of its complacency and a month later, in August 1885, the Criminal Law Amendment Act was passed. The age of consent was raised from 13 to 16 and 'the procurement of girls for prostitution by administering drugs, intimidation or fraud ... [and] the abduction of a girl under 18 for purposes of carnal knowledge' were made criminal offences. Unfortunately, in London, as in Manchester and other cities, the new law did not stop the practice. It simply drove it underground.

In the end, what finally set children free from working in the mills and being trafficked for slaves or sex was not the actions or arguments of women, but the realisation of men that if they were to have a new generation competent to deal with an increasingly technical and changing world, education was an essential key factor. Consequently, a series of Education Acts were brought before Parliament towards the close of the nineteenth century. The 1870 Education Act would provide elementary education for everyone. This was followed by the 1880 Education Act for free compulsory education for children under 10, and the 1899 Education Act raised the age of free compulsory education for children to 12. Finally, it was illegal to force young children to work. Schools were administered by school boards, on which women were allowed to serve, although these were disbanded by the controversial 1902 'Balfour' Act. At this point there were over 2,500 school boards and 14,000 church schools. In 1918 the Fisher Act raised the school leaving age to 14.

Chapter 18

Female Trade Unions

T rade unions were one of the few organisations to benefit in the aftermath of Peterloo. The unions had evolved from crafts guilds of the sixteenth and seventeenth centuries and flourished in the new urban society of mills, manufactories and mines which began to cover England's green and pleasant land during the late eighteenth century. Long hours for low wages in appalling living conditions caused many problems, which workers tried to solve by uniting with their colleagues to fight for their rights. This did not suit either the mill-owning class or the government, who came almost exclusively from an entitled and elite upper class. Consequently, a series of Combination Acts had been passed in 1799 and 1800 which rendered all strike action illegal and punishable by up to three months in prison, or two months' hard labour. This had caused widespread protests and five years after Peterloo the Combination Acts were repealed in 1824 and 1825.

The authorities must have hoped that this would be a sop to all the workers' protests after Peterloo and that the repeals would not cause too much trouble. They were wrong. Long hours and low wages continued to cause trouble, and the government responded through draconian measures to prevent workers from getting together to form trade unions. Matters came to a head in March 1834 when a small trade union of half-a-dozen farmworkers was formed in the Dorset village of Tolpuddle after their wages were reduced by over a third. Agricultural wages were already some of the lowest wages in the country and had been a large part of the reason for country workers flocking to the new towns and mills to seek a better life. The authorities acted with a vengeance by making an example of the six Tolpuddle workers who were arrested and charged with 'administering illegal oaths'. They were then sentenced to transportation to Australia for seven years. This led to a national outcry, a number of marches and protests in support of them, and a mass campaign to free the men who had become known as the 'Tolpuddle Martyrs'. Eventually the authorities backed down and the sentences were pardoned. By 1839 all the 'Tolpuddle Martyrs' had arrived back in England, but they could not settle and five of them eventually emigrated to Canada for the remainder of their lives.

At this point, women were not welcome or involved in trade unions which were considered to be a male-only enclave. Consequently, they began to form their own female unions, although not on the scale or in the numbers of unions for men, after labour unrest reached new levels during the 1830s. In 1832 women organised the first two strikes for equal pay: the women who worked at Robert Owen's 'labour exchange' in London, and card setters in the Yorkshire textile industry at Scholes and Highton. This was followed in 1833 by the Women Power Loom Weavers Association in Glasgow, also on the question of equal pay. In 1834 the Grand National Consolidated Trades Union, which had actively encouraged the establishment of 'lodges of industrious females', took up the cry for equal pay on the grounds that female wages were deliberately kept down by men. The general male response was that equal pay for females would threaten male livelihoods and the tailoring profession even went so far as to say that women should not be allowed to work in their trade.

Women were disappointed that many men seemed to consider that females should work just as hard for much reduced pay and should have no means of protesting this point through a trade union. However, such matters when taken up by women 'were perceived as a serious threat to social cohesion'. During a female mill workers' strike in 1835 a journalist wrote 'that female militancy was 'more menacing to established institutions even than the education of the lower orders'. Once they ventured beyond work such as spinning and weaving – considered extensions of 'womanly duties' – into the factories, women workers were considered a real threat to societal order and moral values. Thinking laterally, many women now threw themselves into supporting Chartism, reasoning that if male enfranchisement was obtained, those men who were sympathetic to their cause for equal pay and the right to belong to a trade union would support them and, in time, achieve results. At this point trade unions were mostly for skilled or better-paid workers, and women, with the exception of those in the weaving trade, were firmly excluded. The general aim of trade unions was, as the secretary of the TUC succinctly put it in 1875, 'to bring about conditions … where wives and daughters would be in their proper sphere at home, instead of being dragged into competition for livelihood against the great and strong men of the world', and the image of the male breadwinner was born, which finally led to married women being barred from employment during the early years of the twentieth century. This writer's grandmother married in 1911, but she could not use her married name so long as she wanted to work, and she had to wear her wedding ring on a chain around her neck under a blouse with a high collar. The greatest irony was that just seven years later, women were keeping the country running by doing all manner of jobs while the men were away fighting in the Great War.

As the Chartism movement had failed and the trade unions had become ever more male orientated one woman finally decided to do something about it. Emma Paterson, born in 1848, the year of the last Chartist petition presentation, was not working class. She was the daughter of a London headmaster who started her working life as an assistant secretary to a union. Emma became interested in female suffrage and had also worked as secretary for the National Society for Women's Suffrage. Subsequently, she founded the Women's Protective and Provident League in 1874, whose aim was to create women-only trade unions in all trades in which women worked, and which they could join for support and protection from exploitation. The League's first female union in 1874 was of bookbinders in London. This was rapidly followed in 1875 by upholsterers, shirt makers and dressmakers, and in 1876 by the Women's Printing Society founded by Emma Paterson herself. She also encouraged the formation of the National Union of Working Women which was based in Bristol; and was the first female delegate to attend a TUC Conference. There was, of course, a considerable amount of male opposition, but she coped because, as one of her male union colleagues put it:

> without either physical attraction or charm, this quiet, shrewd little woman exercised an influence on the Labour movement which no other woman has equalled since her day, and its secret lay in her entire sincerity and absence of pose. She never cared for the limelight, and never thought herself great; but she was great in the truest sense of the word.

Emma Paterson died in 1886, but in 1888 Clementina Black took up the mantle and demands for equal pay for women were once again resolutely on the agenda. A survey by the Journal of the Statistical Society in 1859 had recorded the average wages for cotton operatives in Manchester and Salford:

- average earnings for a man working a 66 hour week (5 × 12 hour days plus Saturday mornings) was 18s 6d (£85.03 in modern values)
- average earnings for a woman working a 66 hour week (5 × 12 hour days plus Saturday mornings) was 10s 2d (£46.70 in modern values)
- average earnings for a boy working a 66 hour week (5 × 12 hour days plus Saturday mornings) was 7s (£32.17 in modern values)
- average earnings for a girl working a 66 hour week (5 × 12 hour days plus Saturday mornings) was 5s (£22.98 in modern values)

A solicitor's daughter from Brighton, Clementina Black was educated at home, but she was fluent in French and German. Although some of her friends were Fabian socialists, she was also close friends with Eleanor Marx, the youngest daughter of Karl Marx, and she was deeply involved with the problems of working-class women and the rapidly evolving Trades Union movement. Clementina became honorary secretary of the Women's Trade Union League in 1886. She clashed frequently with the TUC and helped with the Bryant & May strike in 1888, but she was allowed to attend the Trades Union Congress that year and put forward a motion for equal pay. The seconder of the motion agreed with her and spoke of the gross inequalities for women working in the chain and nail trades. The motion, however, was never acted upon because of the inferior numbers of females within the trade union movement and, consequently, their lack of political influence. Clementina became secretary of the Women's Trade Union League (founded in 1889), which eventually became the Women's Industrial Council, and in 1895 she became editor of the *Women's Industrial News*, the mouthpiece of the Women's Industrial Council. The following year she was among the first to campaign for a legal minimum wage, and by the turn of the century she was also active in several trade union movements.

Chapter 19

Strikes Led by Women

The 1871 Trade Union Act had recognised unions as legal entities entitled to protection under the law, but it was only in 1875 that it had become legal for trade unions to take effective strike action by picketing (Conspiracy and Protection of Property Act 1875). The right to strike was quickly tested when, in February 1875, the Masters' Cartel Association proposed wage cuts for weavers of 2–3 shillings (£6.34 – £9.51 today) per week due to alleged trade fluctuations. In Batley, male and female weavers walked out of Stubley and Taylors Mill, and over in Dewsbury, 300 male and female weavers walked out of Oldroyd's Mill. All the striking weavers conferred and to everyone's utter amazement it was decided that an all-female strike committee was the best option to organise and fight the strike. Here indeed was history in the making. The *Huddersfield Chronicle* for 16 February 1875 didn't know whether to be shocked or astonished. 'Working women coming to the front and taking on labour and there wasn't another place in England where they had done that.'

Thirteen women made up the Dewsbury and Batley Weavers Strike Committee. There were no male members and this firmly established the female voice in trade union activities hitherto closed to women. One of the committee members, Ann Ellis, a power loom weaver, dominated the proceedings. Initially, naturally nervous, she told the Dewsbury newspaper that,

> she had never stood on a platform as she did at present until this strike … she would bundle up and go rather than give in to the masters. If they went in at the reduction the rising generation would have to suffer, and she did not want another

strike but wanted this to do and ... the women had begun the battle and would have to get on with it.

Dewsbury News, 16 February 1875

She continued: 'They could not stand a reduction for rents, rates or coals or flour were dear, as everyone who kept a house would know ... and whilst the masters could live on less profits it was not possible for the workers to live on nothing to eat.' (*Huddersfield Examiner,* 15 February 1875)

The weavers were supported by the loom mechanics who also came out on strike in support and revealed that the masters often cheated female weavers of their due wages by giving them longer warps of yarn to weave than was officially recorded. The weavers then requested help in the form of strike funds from Wakefield miners, Whittaker's Mill in Lancashire and Weemsland Mill in Hawick, as well as from local firms. Over £1,200 (nearly £80,000 today) was raised. Faced with losing profits daily, the masters finally agreed to reinstate weaving prices and wages. The strikers had won. Ironically, Ann Ellis, the leading female voice throughout this strike, died in the dreaded workhouse at Bradford in 1919.

Annie Besant was a London-born Irish girl who was a theosophist; a follower of an ancient Tibetan based religion which believes in 'spiritual emancipation, karma, universal brotherhood and social improvement'. Annie was also a Fabian socialist, writer, speaker, female rights activist, early advocate of birth control, and a member of the London School Board for Tower Hamlets. She counted George Bernard Shaw and Charles Bradlaugh, MP for Northampton and an advocate of universal suffrage, among her friends. Together, Besant and Bradlaugh published a book on birth control which, although they had not personally written it, caused a great scandal, but Annie was no stranger to scandal.

The most notorious women's union strike in British history was probably the Bryant & May matchgirls, who struck successfully for higher wages in 1888. That summer, three Bryant & May matchgirls had been sacked for allegedly talking to a radical journalist – Annie Besant – about the pitifully low wages of 4 shillings (£16.41) per week paid to 16-year-old girls, despite Bryant & May's healthy profits. Annie Besant took up their case and published a story called 'White Slavery in London', about the life of a matchgirl. She wrote,

> The hour for commencing work is 6.30 in summer and 8 in winter; work concludes at 6 p.m. Half-an-hour is allowed for breakfast and an hour for dinner. This long day of work is performed by young girls, who have to stand the whole of the time. A typical case is that of a girl of 16, a piece-worker; she earns 4s. a week. Out of the earnings, 2s. is paid for the rent of one room; the child lives on only bread-and-butter and tea, alike for breakfast and dinner, but related with dancing eyes that once a month she went to a meal where 'you get coffee, and bread and butter, and jam, and marmalade, and lots of it'. The splendid salary of 4s. is subject to deductions in the shape of fines; if the feet are dirty, or the ground under the bench is left untidy, a fine of 3d. is inflicted; for putting 'burnts' – matches that have caught fire during the work.

Bryant & May were furious, first alleging that all their staff were liars as a result of socialist infiltration of the company, and then threatening to sue Annie Besant. Annie stood her ground with the support of the matchgirls. Threats were made to import foreign workers or blacklegs, but the matchgirls held firm, much to the amazement of the management and middle classes, who had not expected such determination or organisation from those they considered feckless and unskilled. The matchgirls stayed out for three weeks, resolutely supported by Annie Besant. At the end of that time the Bryant & May management finally conceded defeat and agreed to almost all their demands.

Margaret Bondfield was born in 1873 at Chard in Somerset; she was of the following generation to Emma Paterson and Clementina Black, but Margaret Bondfield carried on the tradition of strong union women. Her father, William, a lace-maker, was politically active and had been involved with the Anti-Corn Law League during the 1840s. Margaret took an apprenticeship in drapery and embroidery before working as a 'living in' assistant in a number of Brighton drapery shops during the 1890s. Her experience of shop work was not a happy one. She wrote of 'overcrowded, insanitary conditions, poor and insufficient food were the main characteristics of this system, with an undertone of danger … in some houses both natural and unnatural vices found a breeding ground.' In 1894 she moved to London to join her brother, Frank, but found no improvement in shop working conditions. She was expected to work between 80 and 100 hours per week for fifty-one weeks a year.

Under the pen name of Grace Dare, she began writing accounts of the exploitation of shop workers and their grim living and working conditions for the shop workers' magazine *The Shop Assistant*. In 1896 she began working undercover for the Women's Industrial Council by taking jobs in various shops and reporting on every aspect of a shop worker's life. Two years later the Women's Industrial Council published a report on shop workers' conditions based on Bondfield's secret reports. In that same year, 1898, she became assistant secretary of the National Amalgamated Union of Shop Assistants, Warehousemen and Clerks (NASAWC). During this time she met Sydney and Beatrice Webb, and George Bernard Shaw, joined the Fabian Socialists and, later, the Independent Labour Party. She also travelled the country promoting NASAWC and its activities; and in 1899 became the first female delegate to the Trade Union Annual Congress. She worked for NASAWC for ten years before leaving to work for the Women's Labour League (WLL), which she helped to found in 1906. In the same year she helped her best friend, Mary McDonald, to found the National Federation of Women Workers (NFWW) 'dedicated to the unionisation of women workers'. Through them she campaigned for a minimum wage for women of £1 (£78) per week and also for the principle of equal pay for equal jobs.

One of the League's principal aims, alongside promoting the Labour Party, was the direct representation of women in Parliament and on local bodies such as councils. Margot McDonald, the wife of Ramsay McDonald, was the League's president. In 1909, although the Labour Party was committed to including females in suffrage demands, it was unwilling to jeopardise the claims of males not yet enfranchised. As a result, Margaret Bondfield agreed to tone down the WLL motion for female suffrage at the Labour Conference. Although she believed fervently in suffrage for all classes of males and females, she believed in the Labour Party more. However, suffragettes saw her action as a betrayal of great treachery. Nevertheless, since the Qualification of Women Act had been passed in 1907 females had been able to stand as candidates and vote in municipal elections and Margaret stood for Woolwich in both the 1910 and the 1913 London County Council elections. She failed to get elected on either occasion and this may have been as a result of what was seen as her suffragist treachery. Subsequently, she was involved in a national investigation into the working conditions of married women, but she remained closely involved with the WLL. She also helped to investigate minimum wage rates, infant mortality and child welfare. During the Great War she worked as a member of the Women's Peace Council and attended a conference in Bern; but the government, concerned about her possible pacifist attitudes, prevented her from travelling to other conferences in Sweden and America. In 1918 she became the first woman to be elected to the General Council of the TUC, subsequently becoming a Justice of the Peace; in 1923 she became one of the first three female Labour MPs as MP for Northampton. The following year, she became the first female Labour Party minister and, in 1929, the first female cabinet minister and privy councillor.

Margaret Ashton, although a member of the Liberal Party rather than a socialist, was a great supporter of female suffrage and women's rights. She was born at Withington in 1865, one of nine children of Thomas Ashton, a wealthy cotton manufacturer. As a teenager, she helped to raise money for Owen's College (which became the Victoria University of Manchester) and in 1875 she worked voluntarily as the manager of Flowery Fields School in Hyde (now part of Great Manchester). In 1888 she helped to establish the Manchester Women's Guardian Association, which encouraged women to become Poor Law guardians, became interested in politics, and subsequently, in female suffrage, joining the National Union of Women Suffrage Societies (NUWSS). After her father's death in 1898 she increased her political activities and two years later she was elected to Withington Urban District Council. In 1908 she was the first woman to sit on Manchester City Council, where she campaigned on issues of female education, employment and health. Feeling that the Liberals had put female suffrage on the backburner, she resigned from the Liberal Party in 1906 and focused on working hard for the cause of female suffrage, although she distanced herself from the militancy of the WSPU. She was a pacifist and spoke out against the Great War. Consequently condemned as pro-German, she was forced off Manchester City Council in 1921, and as a result, much of her civic work has gone unacknowledged.

Chapter 20

Suffragettes

Suffragettes is often an interchangeable term with suffragists, but in the late nineteenth and early twentieth centuries, suffragettes were suffragists prepared to take militant action to gain women the vote. The call for female suffrage was rapidly growing and it was no surprise that Manchester should lead the way in this respect, for the women of the millscapes had had it tough beyond belief for nearly a century. Now that more men were getting the vote, Manchester women decided that enough was enough. They had supported their men folk towards gaining enfranchisement. Now it was their turn.

The women's suffrage movements had its origins in Manchester, although a group to promote the idea of female suffrage was formed in London in 1866. Lydia Becker was born in Manchester less than eight years after Peterloo, and grew up in the city, believing 'that the notion a husband ought to have … authority over his wife … is the root of all social evils'. She studied botany and astronomy and sometimes contributed to Charles Darwin's scientific work; she also attempted to promote scientific education for girls. In 1866 she heard a lecture on female suffrage given by Barbara Bodichon, who was born in the same year as Lydia Becker. Barbara was a member of a Unitarian radical family from Sussex whose father believed in the rights of women, treating his daughters equally to his sons. Impressed, Lydia Becker was at once converted to the idea of female suffrage and wrote an article about it for the Contemporary Review. The question of women's suffrage was extremely important to her and she lobbied Benjamin Disraeli and *The Spectator* over the enfranchisement of women.

In April 1868, the first public meeting of the National Society for Women's Suffrage took place at the Free Trade Hall in Manchester, where Lydia Becker put forward a resolution that women should have voting rights on the same terms as men. This eventually helped to achieve single women ratepayers being allowed to vote in local council elections through the passing of the Municipal Franchise Act of 1869. It was an important step forward, although it was of little immediate help to the women in the millscapes, since married women were not included until the Local Government Act of 1894, and most did not fulfil the property qualifications anyway. Lydia Becker, however, was on a roll. She toured northern towns and cities, lecturing on behalf of the National Society for Women's Suffrage (NSWS), highlighting the issues and injustices of the voting system, and also campaigning for women to be allowed to serve on school boards. Consequently, she was one of four women, who, in 1870, were elected to serve on the Manchester School Board. It was a huge personal achievement for her and a great opportunity for her to promote her educational ideas. She believed that there was no natural difference between male and female intellects and advocated 'a non-gendered educational system' for Britain. Ten years later she campaigned for the right of women to vote in the House of Keys elections on the Isle of Man. To everyone's utter amazement she succeeded, and women in the Isle of Man voted for the first time in the March elections of 1881; a full thirty-seven years before English women would get the vote. Lydia Becker also provided an early role model for the young Emmeline Pankhurst who is generally credited as a key player in gaining women the vote.

Millicent Garret Fawcett was the daughter of a Suffolk maltster who became mayor of Aldeburgh; her elder sister, Elizabeth Garrett Anderson, became Britain's first female doctor. As a young woman she was greatly influenced by John Stuart Mill, a British philosopher who supported the freedom of the individual over state or social controls and a Liberal MP who staunchly supported female suffrage. In 1866, she collected signatures on the first petition for female suffrage. In 1868, she joined the London Suffrage Committee and spoke at the first female suffrage meeting held in London in 1869. She campaigned for many causes including cruelty towards children, sexually transmitted diseases, and the white slave trade. She admired Lydia Becker, who was a role model for her, as well as for Emmeline Pankhurst. When Lydia Becker died in 1890, the NSWS merged with the National Central Society for Women's Suffrage in London to become the National Union of Women's Suffrage Societies (NUWSS), over which Millicent Garrett Fawcett presided for about twenty years. She wanted to gain suffrage for women through peaceful and legal means, but there was a great deal of party-political prevarication, leading to enormous frustration on the part of NUWSS members and more militant action was proposed by some of them. In 1903, a group led by Emmeline Pankhurst, the Women's Social and Political Union (WSPU), broke away from the NUWSS and began to carry out various acts of sabotage. However, the NUWSS continued in their own way. In 1911, Millicent Fawcett likened the movement to 'a glacier, slow-moving but unstoppable', although it was eventually stopped by the advent of the Great War. All activity ceased and members threw themselves into supporting the war effort in any way needed, even doing the men's jobs while they were away fighting in the trenches and, ironically, it was this which finally won victory for female suffrage.

Emmeline Pankhurst (née Goulden) was born in Moss Side in July 1858. Her mother was Manx and her father a Manchester merchant whose own father had been at Peterloo. When she was 15 she learned of the women's suffrage movement, attending some of their talks and meetings, through which she met Richard Pankhurst, a barrister and a keen supporter of women's suffrage. He was twenty-four years older than her, but they married in 1879 and had five children by 1889. Unusually for the times, he did not expect her to stay at home. Instead he fully supported her political and suffrage activities. One of her friends was Keir Hardie, a Scotsman who was a Fabian socialist. The Fabians (of whom Sidney and Beatrice Webb, both economists and socialists, were notable members) were a society of socialists initially formed in 1884 to promote democratic socialism through gradual reforms within democracies. There was, however, a certain degree of intellectual snobbery and Fabian socialists did not want working-class women to have the vote, only those of the upper and middle classes. While Emmeline and Christabel Pankhurst both agreed with the principles of the Fabian Socialists, Sylvia Pankhurst did not, and nor did the youngest Pankhurst sister, Adela. Sylvia eventually became a Socialist and went to live and work among the poor working-class women of East London. A few years after Richard Pankhurst's death, Adela was forced by her mother to emigrate to Australia.

In 1888, the NSWS, then led by Lydia Becker and Millicent Fawcett, split after a number of members agreed to affiliate with organisations connected to political parties. The two leaders subsequently formed their own breakaway group called the Parliament Street Society (PPS), and Emmeline Pankhurst joined this society. However, some members felt married women 'did not need the vote, as their husbands would vote for them', and that votes for single women and widows should be the initial approach. As a result, the following year Emmeline and Richard Pankurst set up yet another new society, the Women's Franchise League (WFL), which would fight for the vote for all women. The WFL was considered to be quite radical because it also supported equal rights for women in matters of divorce and inheritance as well encouraging trade unionism.

Richard Pankhurst died in 1898, and in 1903 Emmeline Pankhurst and her daughters, together with Manchester cotton worker Annie Kenney, decided to establish the Women's Social and Political Union (WSPU) because they felt that social and electoral reforms were too long overdue and that more militant efforts might be needed to obtain them.

Suffragette and social justice campaigner Esther Roper met the Irish upper-class poet and playwright Eva Gore-Booth in 1896 and the pair became firm friends. They bought a small terraced cottage at Rusholme in Manchester, and together they worked for the twin causes of social justice and women's suffrage. In 1903, together with

Manchester-born suffragette and trade unionist, Sarah Reddish, who was active in the Co-operative movement, they helped to establish the Lancashire and Cheshire Women's Textile and Other Workers Representation Committee. This organisation supported the campaign in nearby Wigan of Hubert Sweeney, who was standing for Parliament as a candidate for women's suffrage. Eva, meantime, had become a member of the National Union of Women's Suffrage Societies. She worked in Ancoats on behalf of working-class women and subsequently became co-secretary of the Manchester and Salford Women's Trade Union Council. In 1904 Christabel Pankhurst tried to make women's suffrage one of the aims of this council, but they refused, which led to the resignation of Eva Gore-Booth. Together with Sarah Dickenson, who had also resigned, she set up the Manchester and Salford Women's Trade and Labour Council, which did support the suffrage cause. Sarah Dickenson had been born in Hulme, one of the city's inner and more deprived suburbs. She had worked in the cotton mills since the age of 11 and was passionate about the cause of female suffrage.

In 1905 Esther became secretary of the National Industrial and Professional Women's Suffrage Society, while Eva continued her work for both the suffrage cause and for the rights of working-class women. For a short time in 1911 she worked at the pit head of a Manchester coal mine so that she was fully conversant with the low wages and generally undesirable working conditions which working-class women endured. It also gave her a glimpse of what it was like to be a working-class woman in a heavily industrialised city at the beginning of the twentieth century. However, both Esther and Eva distanced themselves from the Women's Social and Political Union (WSPU) run by Emmeline Pankhurst, because they disagreed with the use of militancy and they also felt that Emmeline ignored the problem of working-class women's rights.

Annie Kenney was one of twelve children, she was a mill-girl from Saddleworth on the outskirts of Manchester. She had begun working in the mills part-time when she was 10 and was working full-time twelve-hour shifts by the time she was 13. Annie was a weaver's assistant and part of her work involved fitting bobbins and dealing with broken strands of yarn when they occurred. When she was about 15 years old, one of her fingers was amputated by a spinning bobbin in an accident. Compensation was not often paid and there was no sick pay, but Annie was undaunted. She stayed working at the mill for fifteen years and became involved in trade union activities. She also read a great deal, thereby furthering her own education, achieving the distinction of becoming, in 1912, the only working-class woman in the hierarchy of the WSPU. The WSPU colours were white, green and purple, and they explained the reasons for their choices:

> purple ... is the royal colour ... and stands for the royal blood that flows in the veins of every suffragette, the instinct of freedom and dignity ... white stands for purity in private and public life ... green is the colour of hope and the emblem of spring.

Hannah Mitchell was one of six children born to a farming family in the bleak but romantic surroundings below Alport Castles in Hope Woodlands near Manchester, she became a dedicated socialist and suffragette, and a member of the WSPU. She wrote her autobiography, *The Hard Way*, with instructions that it was not to be published until after her death. Hannah worked as a seamstress in Manchester, speaking publicly at meetings of the Independent Labour Party (ILP), while also working part-time for the WSPU. She recognised very clearly the dilemma faced by women who had to work for a living, care for their family, and take part in any other activities such as supporting the fight for female suffrage. 'No cause can be won between dinner and tea', she wrote, 'and most of us who were married had to work with one hand tied behind us.' In 1907, Hannah suffered a nervous breakdown – partly due to over-working, partly to malnourishment – and was hurt by the fact that none of the Pankhurst family visited her when she was ill. As a pacifist, however, she was not entirely at ease with WSPU policies and left the WSPU in 1908.

Christabel Pankhurst, her mother Emmeline's favourite, was a pretty, intelligent girl and, like her sisters, had attended Manchester High School for Girls. She took a law degree at Manchester University, but being female, she was not allowed to practice law. Women were not allowed to practise law because a court had ruled that 'women were not persons' (Bebb v Law Society 1913 application for women to become solicitors). The passing of the Sex Disqualification (Removal) Act 1919 removed that distinction by stating that,

> a person shall not be disqualified by sex or marriage from the exercise of any public function, or from being appointed to or holding any civil or judicial office or post, or from entering or assuming or carrying on any civil profession or vocation, or for admission to any incorporated society.

Christabel was upset, but worked hard for the suffrage cause – although she disagreed with her sister, Sylvia, that working-class women should be involved. She preferred middle- and upper-class women 'of greater intelligence', who were prepared to use militant tactics. When the Great War broke out, Emmeline and Christabel became increasingly right wing and campaigned hard for military involvement and conscription, while Sylvia remained a left-wing pacifist. After the war, Christabel stood as a Woman's Party candidate in the December 1918 elections – the first in which women could vote – and lost narrowly to the Labour candidate. Disillusioned, she left England for the United States in 1921.

Sylvia Pankhurst (born Estelle Sylvia), distanced herself physically from Emmeline and Christabel, and moved to London in 1917 to work among the poorest inhabitants of the East End. She became a socialist, then a communist and vociferous pacifist, which annoyed Emmeline intensely, who saw it as an act of the utmost treachery. Sylvia had no intention of being forced to emigrate like her sister Adela and remained in London after the war, championing the cause of the working class. She suffered from her mother's criticisms and finally openly defied her by refusing to get married. She gave birth to an illegitimate son, Richard, in 1927, but Emmeline had always clung to certain social standards of behaviour and consequently refused ever to speak to Sylvia again. Sylvia then decided on emigration herself and took her son to Addis Ababa, where she spent much of the rest of her life working for the poor and under-privileged. Richard Pankhurst grew up to become a distinguished academic, a professor at the University of Addis Ababa, and a founding member of the Institute of Ethiopian Studies. His daughter, Dr Helen Pankhurst, still works hard for the female cause.

A surprising but important and active supporter of female suffrage was Indian princess Sophia Duleep Singh, a daughter of Duleep Singh, the last Maharaja of the Punjab, and a goddaughter of Queen Victoria. She grew up at the family home in the Suffolk village of Elveden. Her father had been separated from his mother as a boy and brought to exile in Britain after the annexation of the Punjab in 1849. He was then made to present his birthright of the fabulous Koh-i-Noor diamond to Queen Victoria. In the early years of the twentieth century, one of Sophia's brothers, Prince Frederick Duleep Singh, bought a fourteenth-century manor house on the Norfolk-Suffolk borders and Sophia spent some time there with him and her eldest sister, Princess Bamba. In woodlands bordering the grounds of his home, Prince Frederick built a small Indian temple. Set back from the road and hidden by trees, it was a quiet, pretty and lonely spot where he and his sisters could pay secret homage to their lost homeland. Subsequently, on a trip to India in 1907, Sophia saw the poverty inflicted on her family and the Indian sub-continent by the British Raj, and by the time she returned to England in 1909, she did not appreciate either the Empire or the way it treated its women. Consequently, she became a friend of the Pankhursts and joined the WSPU. She also refused to pay her taxes in protest and authorised a sale of some of her belongings, the proceeds of which she donated to the Women's Tax Resistance League. Her title of Princess was useful to the suffragettes as well as her grace and favour apartment at Hampton Court Palace. Although she was fined for misdemeanours she was never arrested, the authorities mindful of possible adverse publicity and scandal. During the Great War she nursed Indian soldiers evacuated from the Western Front, and in 1934 she declared her life's purpose to be the advancement of women.

There was huge support for the objectives of equal rights in divorce and inheritance matters among Manchester women, despite the Married Women's Property Act passed in 1882. This long-awaited Act had finally restored a woman's legal identity as separate to that of her husband, and her right to own her land, her property, and her earnings herself. They no longer belonged to her husband, and nor did any inheritance she might receive. However, while this was a big step forward, Manchester women were no longer content to be regarded as second-class citizens. Too many female lives had been stunted and wasted. They wanted total control over their own lives and to be part of the political process. Universal suffrage would give them that power. However, there were concerns that many women would be 'unsexed by emancipation'. On the surface it seems a strange idea that having the vote should 'unsex' a woman, but that was not what was really meant. Men understood only too well that female suffrage would accord women more status, as well as more power and more control over their lives. Queen Victoria, although enjoying and making thorough use of her own status, power and control, seemed to share this view that females, with, of course, the sole exception of the queen herself, should not have any form of equality with men. She did not say so publicly, but she wrote in 1870 to Theodore Martin, that the question of female suffrage,

> is a subject which makes the Queen so furious that she cannot contain herself ... God created men and women different ... then let them remain each in their own position ... woman would become the most hateful heartless and disgusting of

human beings were she allowed to unsex herself; and where would be the protection which man was intended to give the weaker sex?

It was a savage indictment totally lacking in empathy and understanding.

Some countries of the queen's empire clearly did not share her views. In 1893, New Zealand became the 'first self-governing country in the world to introduce female suffrage'. The campaign was centred in Christchurch and led by a woman named Kate Shepherd. Many folk in New Zealand were in favour of female suffrage because

> a democratic government like that of New Zealand ... admits the great principle that every adult person, not convicted of crime, not suspected of lunacy, has an inherent right to a voice in the construction of the laws [and] because it has not yet been proved that the intelligence of women is only equal to that of children nor that their social status is on a par with that of lunatics or convicts.

One of the most important campaigners for female suffrage was a Maori woman. Meri Te Tai Mangakahia also campaigned for women to be eligible to sit in the Maori parliament. Her arguments were essentially the same as those of Kate Shepherd and her followers. She also pointed out that there were numbers of women who were either widowed or had no male members in their family, and some who were wealthy owned land and knew how to manage it. On 19 September 1893, both European and Maori women were enfranchised. It was a huge victory, but one that women in Manchester could only read about and envy deeply because their efforts at attaining the same goal were being seriously hampered.

The granting of female suffrage in Britain

There still remained plenty of male opposition to female suffrage, as might be expected, but female opposition was much harder to understand. Most of it came from upper-class women. Novelist Mary Ward (better known as Mrs Humphry Ward ... she insisted on using his name to show that she was 'utterly and voluntarily her husband's property') published 'An Appeal Against Women's Suffrage' in 1889, insisting that 'a woman's sphere should be entirely domestic'. Like Beatrice Webb, she was not keen on the idea of any woman 'not well educated, intelligent or affluent' having any power. She made the common mistake of confusing intelligence with education, and affluence was still the name of the class game. She was endorsed in her views by Mrs Frederic Harrison who published articles in 'Queen' and felt that 'female suffrage ... must cut into the peace and well-being of families and re-act for harm on the education of children'. In Manchester, Mrs Arthur Somervell, wife of English composer, Arthur Somervell, gave a speech in which she stated that 'the burden of womanhood is necessarily motherhood which is at once her burden and her glory'. Margot Asquith, wife of the prime minister, H.H. Asquith, was particularly bitter and vitriolic in her attacks and continually derided suffragettes as 'wombless, vicious, cruel women'. She was a woman who believed that most women, but especially working-class women, were 'intellectually inferior to herself'. Supporters of the vote for women were castigated as 'embittered spinsters, ignorant and stupid'. The male opposition, however, displayed even more disdain, and an actual dislike of their womenfolk that had not been evident in the New Zealand suffrage campaign, despite the best efforts of Henry Fish, MP for Dunedin on South Island. British men claimed that,

women were psychologically and mentally unfit to make important political decisions ... too ruled by emotion and debilitated by menstruation and childbirth to be able to vote with a clear head ... women's suffrage would lead to a neglect of husbands and children and to ... the total breakdown of society.' A number of male artists caricatured women as 'deranged lunatics with misshapen heads, Neanderthal-style features, unkempt hair and crazed expressions on their faces ... [with] the words 'we want the vote'.

Such derision and condemnation backfired, however, because as Christabel Pankhurst noted, the extremity of it simply encouraged support for the female suffrage cause.

The Liberal party had proclaimed themselves great supporters of female suffrage, but in the early years of the twentieth century Liberal governments procrastinated, and progress in female enfranchisement practically ceased. This caused enormous resentment and frustration among suffragettes, which led in 1904 to some taking militant action, breaking windows, pouring corrosive liquids into post-boxes, setting fires, cutting telegraph wires and later, in 1913, bombing the home of David Lloyd George. This caused serious divisions within the suffragette movement because many, including Emmeline Pankhurst's daughters, Sylvia and Adela, felt that violent means were wrong. In 1906 a Liberal government was elected and 400 of the 650 MPs were in favour of female suffrage, but it ran out of time in 1907 and did not become law. In 1909 another Bill was introduced which proposed suffrage for all males and some females, but was dropped when a new election was called over budget matters.

A similar Bill was reintroduced in 1910, but dropped again when yet another election was called. In 1911 a Bill to give at least some females the vote was passed with a large majority but the Liberal Prime Minister, H.H. Asquith, changed his mind, dropped the Bill, and introduced a new one which simply gave the vote to more classes of men. Despite his indication that it could be amended to give some women the vote, the Speaker ruled that a Bill for male suffrage could not be used to enfranchise women. The fury and resentment this deliberate prevarication induced led to an increase in militant acts by suffragettes, many of whom were arrested and badly treated by the authorities. The WSPU seemed to be set on a collision course with the government, but Emmeline didn't care. WSPU members protested loudly at public events. They smashed windows, threw stones, set fire to post-boxes, and assaulted police officers. Perpetrators were arrested and imprisoned, but staged hunger strikes to draw attention to their plight as well as campaigning for better conditions in prisons. One of them, Emily Wilding Davison, a militant London suffragette, attracted international notoriety and earned her place in the history books when she ran onto the racecourse during the Derby in June 1913 and tried to pin suffragette colours on 'Anmer', the king's horse, as a protest against the continued delays in granting female suffrage. However, she miscalculated the speed and power of the horse and she was fatally injured, much to the disapproving horror of King George V and Queen Mary.

Militant suffragettes, led by Emmeline Pankhurst, would regularly go on hunger strike after being arrested. At first the authorities let them go home when their condition became weakened and serious, but subsequently it was decided that hunger strikers should be force fed. Force feeding was brutal, degrading and extremely painful. Women were physically held down by force or straps and their jaws forced open by a cloth or steel gag. A long thin tube was then violently pushed up their nose or down their throat and a jug of liquid poured down the tube. Victims complained of unbearable pain, drowning sensations and repeated gagging. Hygiene was practically non-existent and several women ended up becoming seriously ill. For some, this practice shortened their lives.

Emmeline Pethick-Lawrence – who had done social work in the East End of London like Sylvia Pankhurst – and her husband Frederick, were both active members of the WSPU and founded 'Votes for Women' in 1907. In 1912 they were arrested and imprisoned for breaking windows in WSPU demonstrations. They did not go on hunger strike but just served their sentences. Neither of them approved of the increasingly militant tactics and said so. Consequently, they were ejected from the WSPU by Emmeline and Christabel Pankhurst.

In the end, however, it was not radicals or female suffrage supporters, or any individual or organisation, which finally won women in Britain the vote. It was the Great War (1914–1918). On the declaration of war, all the women's organisations ceased campaigning for their individual objectives and threw their time and energies into supporting the war effort. At first it was mainly back-up support they provided, but as more and more men were called up, women began to take over the men's jobs which they did with equal effectiveness and efficiency, much to the total amazement of most men. There was resistance initially; female shop assistants and tram conductresses were abused, both verbally and physically. Farmers refused to employ Land Girls to work in the place of their male farmhands, female drivers were jeered and there was a lot of sneering that women would not manage any job that was physically taxing. Finally, men were forced to admit that on all counts, women could perform tasks as well as any man and, on several counts, better than the men. In the face of these female achievements, which had proved the doomsayers wrong, and admitting that women were as well equipped, both intellectually and psychologically, as most men to deal with anything, Parliament decided that it could no longer withhold the right to vote from women. In 1918, almost a century after the bloody carnage and nightmare of Peterloo, the Representation of the People Act gave the vote to virtually all men and to all women over the age of 30. This was followed by universal suffrage granted just ten years later in 1928, which gave all men and women over the age of 21 (now 18) the right to vote. Women were jubilant. They had worked so long for this day. The writer Virginia Woolf, who helped to found the Bloomsbury Set and the Hogarth press, and herself a keen supporter of women's rights and higher education for women, announced that it was now the remit of every female writer to 'kill the angel in the house', the meek, yielding, self-sacrificing, completely subjugated version of womanhood as envisaged by Coventry Patmore (see p.10).

Chapter 21

Parliament

It was a long weary road from Peterloo that had finally led to women taking their seats in the House of Commons, but it was also an amazing transition – from females not even being recognised as 'persons', to becoming equals to men, with the right to vote and to take their place in Parliament, within a single century or just four generations.

Nancy, Viscountess Astor, was the first female MP to sit in the English House of Commons, but ironically, she was American born and bred. She had moved to England in 1905 and married Waldorf Astor in 1906. They owned the Cliveden estate in Buckinghamshire and a house on St James Square in London. She became a society hostess and believed in the expansion of British imperialism. When Waldorf Astor's father died in 1919, he succeeded to the title of Viscount Astor and automatically received a seat in the House of Lords, which meant he had to relinquish his parliamentary constituency seat of Plymouth Sutton in the House of Commons. Nancy Astor decided to contest her husband's seat in a by-election held on 28 November 1919 and subsequently took up her seat in the Commons as a confirmed Conservative member. She was not the first female MP to be elected, however. That honour belonged to Constance Markievicz, the sister of Eva Gore Booth, who was elected for Dublin St Patricks in 1918 but she did not take her seat in the Commons because, along with other Sinn Féin members, she helped to form the first Dáil Éireann. She said of Nancy Astor that she was 'of the upper classes and out of touch'.

Although she had not been a suffragette, Nancy Astor was welcomed by the suffragette movement, but not by many of her male colleagues who jeered and blocked her passage when she first attended the Commons. She rallied further support for her quick wit and improvisation, and through her work with charities and Canadian soldiers during the Great War. After taking her seat in the Commons in 1919, Nancy quickly made an enemy of Horatio Bottomley MP when she opposed divorce reform, which he considered gross hypocrisy as she had divorced her first husband, an American named Robert Shaw. In time she made friends with Margaret Wintringham, a British female MP elected in 1921, and Ellen Wilkinson, a Manchester-born Labour MP who would later go on to become minister of education. Nancy Astor was not a particularly popular person. She was noted for her sharp tongue and for her efforts at getting the age for drinking alcohol raised from 14 to 18. She also attracted a lot of criticism for her anti-Catholic and anti-Communism stances, and for her obvious dislike of Jewish people. She eventually resigned from her parliamentary seat in 1945.

Margaret Wintringham was born in a small village near Keighley in West Yorkshire in 1879. Her father was a teacher and Margaret trained as a teacher as well, eventually becoming head of a school in Grimsby and a member of Grimsby Education Board. She took a keen interest in women's issues and was involved in various organisations including the National Union of Women Workers and the Liberal Party. Her husband became MP for Louth in Lincolnshire and, after his death in 1921, she replaced him as the Liberal candidate in the local by-election and won, becoming the first female Liberal MP, the third woman elected to the House of Commons, and the first British born female MP.

Epilogue and The Bicentenary of Peterloo 2019

Beneath the modern paving slabs of St Peter's Square lie the remains of a hidden graveyard, marked only by a cross opposite the main public entrance to Central Library. Under the neat clean twenty-first century façade of the square there are a number of graves, and the Birley family crypt containing the tomb of Hugh Hornby Birley, the harsh elitist mill owner who led the charge of the Manchester Yeomanry at Peterloo. Although twenty were killed and almost 700 injured as his sabre-wielding cavalry charged into an unarmed crowd, Birley, convinced of his entitled and elite righteousness, never really understood the crime that had been committed against the people of Manchester. He died in August 1845 and did not live to see the reform and revolution which Peterloo had instigated.

Women had finally won the vote in 1918 after the Great War and universal suffrage followed ten years later in 1928. Constituencies were equal and MPs were paid. Although it had not happened immediately, the protests of Peterloo and the harsh authoritarian reaction were the catalyst for a chain of events and reforms through the nineteenth century, which had eventually resulted in a democratic Parliament, universal suffrage, the recognition and implementation of workers' rights and social justice, with equal opportunities for all in education and employment. Women virtually had equal rights, if not equal pay. Children under 12 were no longer allowed to work. However, by the time of the Peterloo centenary in 1919, the country had only just emerged from the 'war to end all wars', and was in the grip of a lethal flu pandemic. No one had either the energy or the resources to celebrate the centenary of Peterloo, except for a small commemorative booklet written by an assistant master at Manchester Grammar School. Folk promised themselves that Peterloo would not be forgotten, but much of the burning enthusiasm had waned now that the objectives of universal suffrage, social justice, better pay, more educational and career opportunities had been achieved by the women of the nineteenth century, who had fought so hard for their place alongside men. There would be other celebrations in the future. It was a brave new world.

It should have been a progressive time, but the war and the broken promises of a 'land fit for heroes' had taken their toll, resulting in banking crises, recession, strikes, unemployment, poverty and hunger. It was an extraordinarily difficult time for many people.

Just twenty years after the Great War, which had earned women the vote, there was another, even more viciously destructive war, which lasted six long years. After the horrors of the Second World War, the late 1950s and the 1960s were seen as a golden era. Successive Conservative governments, notably those of Harold Macmillan and Sir Anthony Eden, repeatedly told the working classes 'You've never had it so good'. Women tested out their new-found freedoms and opportunities in education, employment and lifestyle with enthusiasm. The advent of birth control meant they could now decide when, or if, to have children. However, there were still women who could not, or would not, vote independently of their husbands. It became common and socially acceptable for women who married not to go out to work, even if they had no children, which led to male accusations of simply being seen as meal tickets. Peterloo was not on the school curricula, was neither taught nor talked about any longer. Those who were there and those who had followed and struggled so valiantly for female recognition and universal suffrage were dead. Peterloo seemed all but forgotten, except on the streets of Manchester, where it was made clear to local police forces that attempts to use mounted police for maintaining law and order would cause civil unrest. The folk memory remained so strong for Mancunians that it would be over 150 years after Peterloo before mounted police could patrol the streets of the city.

The Greek historian Thucydides always maintained that history was cyclical. People did not learn from their predecessors or previous events. Although he was writing 400 years before the birth of Christ, he lived in the democracy of Athens, which was fairly permanently at war with its more military and far less democratic neighbour of Sparta, as well as with other Greek states, jealous of Athens' success, sophistication and wealth. Thucydides, like many of his compatriots, believed in democracy and a free vote, but like his counterparts of over 2,000 years later, he only believed in these privileges for the 'upper orders', not for the 'lower orders'. The 'upper orders' were defined much as the 'upper classes' are today in Britain, on grounds of rank, wealth and ancestry. Many of the 'lower orders' were slaves, but there was an important difference between these slaves and modern slave workers. Athenian slaves could work their way out of slavery to become respected 'freedmen', accorded certain civil privileges. Millions of others down the centuries have not been so lucky and this has led to wars and strife across the world. The 'slaves' of the Industrial Revolution, and its aftermath, would never have an option to work their way out of anything, and although the British had abolished slavery in theory in 1833, in practice they had not. The 'upper orders' still took the view that if the 'lower orders' were poor, it was because they were underpaid and under-privileged and that was their own fault, because they were simply lower persons of lesser intelligence who could not earn a decent living. Therefore, the situation did not require any rectification. Although many of the 'upper orders' had received an education in the 'Classics', they had not learned the lessons either.

As the twentieth century progressed, voter turnout at general elections fell from 84 per cent in 1950 to 59 per cent in 2001, while local elections struggled to reach 45 per cent. 'Use it or lose it' became the mandatory cry against voter apathy. The need to dismiss and disrespect workers reared its head once more in the twenty-first century; much of it after the banking crash of 2008, but especially in the summer of 2018 when the Conservative Prime Minister, Theresa May, stated that workers earning under £50K were not skilled (and by implication not worth much), which caused a huge outcry as many low paid jobs involve medical posts, teaching, librarians, social workers, pharmacists, and vets (*New Statesman*, 3 October 2018).

Women's pay in many spheres has remained lower than that of men, clearly evidenced by the question of the pay differentials between male and female presenters working for the BBC. The Fawcett Society (named after Millicent Fawcett) studied statistics from the Office of National Statistics (ONS) gained from the Annual Survey of Hours and Earnings (ASHE) and discovered that 'the mean gap in gender pay for full time workers is 13.1%'. If part-time workers are included the differential rises to 16.2 per cent. The 'glass ceiling', which so many women have complained about since the 1960s, remains firmly in place, ensuring that females generally do not progress beyond a certain level, either professionally or financially, in their chosen careers. There is also evidence, according to the Fawcett Society, that a growing number of younger men feel that 'women's equality has gone too far'. The spectre of 'zero hours' contracts, with their restrictive conditions, first introduced in 1999, also displayed a complete lack of understanding of the need for people to earn a regular living wage. Low wages are still paid for much of the work done in Britain, especially for those jobs seen as 'women's work', thereby increasing poverty levels (Joseph Rowntree Organisation, 2015; The UN 2018). Those at the time of Peterloo had suffered reduced working hours or unemployment, but did not expect to be forbidden to try and find other interim work as is the case with many zero hours contracts. It was hoped that the twenty-first century would herald a new positive era. The signs had been promising until apathy set in. Younger females began taking their hard-won privileges for granted. Young people of both sexes declared that 'they couldn't be bothered to vote' because 'nothing ever changes does it'. At the same time the 'upper orders' once again began to reinforce the notion that poverty is the fault of the poor, victim blaming for poor decisions and thereby obviating the need for anything to be done about it. Therefore, the bicentenary of Peterloo in 2019 was looked upon as an opportunity for once again highlighting social injustices.

The commemoration took place on 16 August 2019 in Manchester, where it all began on the site of St Peter's Field. By this time, however, the wheel seemed to have turned full circle because the same requests as 1819 were now being repeated due to a proposed intention to suspend Parliament for an unspecified length of time; a dual voting system (declared illegal in 1867) in place to elect a new prime minister; a proposal that voter ID would be necessary for people to vote in local or national elections, thereby destroying the principle of the secret ballot, as well as unequal pay for numbers of women, zero hour contracts and low wages, eliciting pleas for a 'fair day's pay for a fair day's work'. The ceremony itself was simple and moving. Many social groups took part and there was marching, music, singing, poetry, and silences for remembrance. It was a reaffirmation of the spirit of Peterloo. At the end, the names of those who had died at Peterloo were solemnly read out. Manchester saw the parallels between 1819 and 2019 and the city was quick to support the bicentenary commemoration with events, exhibitions, guided tours, public debates, concerts, street and theatre performances, through the visual arts and a permanent memorial, which will stand at Manchester Central on the former site of St Peter's Field. The profile was further raised by *The Guardian* debates on current affairs (held in Central Library also on the site of St Peter's Field) because it was due to Peterloo that *The Guardian* (then the *Manchester Guardian*) was born in 1821.

Twelve days after the commemoration of Peterloo 2019 the unthinkable happened.

The Conservative Prime Minister, Boris Johnson, announced that Parliament would be suspended, initially for a minimum of five weeks, to force through controversial legislation. This move effectively prevented all Parliamentary debate and disenfranchised both MPs and ordinary voters. Not even Lord Liverpool, the Conservative Prime Minister of 1819, had ever considered such a measure. The population of 2019 was stunned, and the ghosts of parliamentary politics past shivered in their graves. What had Peterloo 1819 been about? 'History is cyclical.' Thucydides' words echoed back down the centuries. Those who could fight back, did so, and after two weeks the Supreme Court of the United Kingdom overturned the prime minister's decision and ordered Parliament to be reinstated. This caused a great deal of anger and bitterness on the part of many Conservative MPs. Despite the protestations of the Speaker, vitriolic invective was used in the House of Commons (Hansard 25 September 2019), designed to incite hatred and prejudice among both MPs and the public.

Further echoes of 1819 occurred as females involved in politics were threatened with verbal abuse, assault, and threats of rape, sexual mutilation, or death (as reported on BBC News website 4 November 2019). These complaints, however, were dismissed as 'humbug' by the prime minister (House of Commons and Hansard 25 September 2019). Female politicians were targeted with accusations by some male members of the crowd outside Westminster, that they were simply 'whores' (BBC evening news 26 September 2019). It was a shocking repetition of the accusations levelled at women in 1819 by hostile newspapers, like the *Manchester Courier* and the *Manchester Comet*, or cartoonists such as George Cruickshank.

In late October 2019 a general election was called for 12 December. There are 650 seats in the House of Commons. Only 208 (less than one third) are held by women. Nineteen of these women (approx. 9 per cent) resigned their seats, with most citing the constant abuse and threats as a main or contributing factor. By contrast, thirty-nine males (approx. 8.5 per cent) resigned for a variety of reasons including retirement, having the Party whip withdrawn or pursuing other interests; none of them cited threats or abuse (BBC News 31 October 2019). All Parliamentary candidates for the forthcoming December election were 'advised by the police and Parliament not to canvas alone; not to be out after dark; not to enter constituents' homes; and to carry a panic alarm at all times.' This warning applied most particularly to female candidates and canvassers (*The Observer*, 3 November 2019). The general consensus in 1819 was what else did women expect, and that they should just 'shut up and put up'. Although the situation of women is rather different in 2019, the repressions, cruelties and taunts of 1819 are being repeated with the same intentions, proving that true female emancipation has yet to come. Nineteenth-century attitudes towards women are still there, still simmering, just below the surface. However, the cruellest irony was that the Conservative Party Conference of 2019 was held in Manchester Central on the site of the Peterloo Massacre, where so many women suffered so much in the fight for freedom, social justice, democracy and the right of everyone to vote.

Appendix: Female Freedom Expressed in Fashion After the Victorian Era

Women now had unparalleled freedoms, which their grandmothers and great-grandmothers in the Peterloo era could only have dreamed about. They could vote. They could receive higher education. They could work in a variety of jobs. They could own their own property and their own bodies. Birth-control was still a new concept but would soon give women even greater choices and freedoms. They did not yet have total equality, but that would come – they hoped. One of the newest freedoms they enjoyed was the lack of severely restrictive clothing, largely due to the efforts of the Rational Dress Movement. The movement had first emerged in the 1850s as women had begun slowly gaining concessions. It supported women's education and suffrage causes and called for an end to fashion dictates supposedly designed only to please men. The unwieldy wire hoops of the crinoline, the outlandishness of the bustle, and the restrictive horrors of tight-laced corsets, posed the greatest threats to female health. Crinolines were both accident-prone and a terrible fire risk; the bustle to a lesser extent, but whalebone corsets could damage internal organs, affect fertility and induce general poor health and weakness. Some argued that a decent corset was essential for stylish dress and good posture. Others believed that female attractiveness was defined by a firm corset and a 'wasp waist'. This writer wore a whalebone corset for three days while working as a film extra. It was uncomfortable, restrictive, painful after eating lunch, unbearable by teatime, and the points dug sharply and painfully into vulnerable thighs. The resulting bruises took a month to heal.

After the Great War new, much less restrictive female clothing came into fashion, including the liberty bodice (a sleeveless buttoned vest); bloomers (knickers fastened or elasticated just above or below the knee and named after Amelia Bloomer who invented the style); loose dresses with dropped waists (so popular with 1920s women); wide-leg trousers for women (full length bloomers but not usually gathered at the ankle). These changes brought forth the usual expected complaints: 'Women were losing their femininity and mystique by abandoning long flowing clothing.' Critics of women's rights saw wearing trousers as a 'usurpation of male authority'. The clergy, not unnaturally, believed it would all lead to a fall in moral standards. Women mostly ignored them. Comfort, ease of movement and good health had become more important. It was a new era and freedoms which had been hard won were to be cherished. The long struggle for female recognition since Peterloo had finally been won.

Timelines
Politics
1678   Tory party first formed

1678   Whig party first formed

1834   Tories become modern Conservative Party

1859   Liberal Party formed from Whigs, Peelite supporters, Radicals and the Independent Irish Party

1893   ILP founded by Keir Hardie

1900   Labour Party founded by Keir Hardie

Chartism
1838   Peoples' Charter

1839   Chartists' First Petition

1842   Chartists' Second Petition

1849   Chartists' Third Petition

Parliamentary representation and the right to enfranchisement

1832 The Great Reform Act

1867 The Second Reform Act

1868 First female suffrage society formed

1872 Voting by secret ballot

1884 The Third Reform Act

1885 Redistribution of Parliamentary Seats Act

1897 Merger of two main female suffrage societies

1917 Representation of the People Act gives the vote to most males and a large number of females

1928 Representation of the People Act gives universal suffrage to all males and females

Women's Rights

1839 Custody of Infants Act ... mothers could petition for custody of under 7s and access to over 7s

1853 Aggravated Assaults Act passed to reduce cases of wife beating but has limited success

1857 Matrimonial Causes Act by which civil divorce becomes legal

1869 *The Subjection of Women* is published demanding equal rights for women

1869 Municipal Franchise Act

1870 Women get the vote in the Isle of Man

1870 Married Women's Property Act

1870 Women elected to School Boards created under the 1870 Elementary Education Act

1875 Women elected as Poor Law Guardians

1883 Women given virtual equality with men over property rights and protection

1894   Local Government Act

1907   Qualification of Women Act 1907

1913   Appeal Court judge rules 'a woman is not a person' in legal application

1917   Large numbers of females awarded the right to vote

1918   Representation of the People Act passed giving women over the age of 30 the right to vote

1918   Parliament (Qualification of Women) Act

1918   Constance Markievicz (Irish Republic) first female MP elected

1919   Sex Disqualification (Removal) Act

1919   Nancy Astor (American) first female MP to take seat in House of Commons

1921   Margaret Wintringham first English female MP

1928   Representation of the People Act giving universal suffrage

Employment conditions after Peterloo

1819   Cotton Mills and Factories Act/Twelve Hours Act

1833   Factory Act: no children under 9 to work in factories (except silk mills); children under 13 to work no more than nine hours per day; under 18s not to work nights

1842   Act bans women and boys from working underground

1844   Factory Act covering textile factories bans all children under eight from working; women and children to work a maximum twelve hours a day

1847   Ten Hours Act banning women and children working more than ten hours a day

1867   Factory Acts Extension applies existing laws to all factories employing over fifty persons

1867   Workshops Regulation Act factory laws applied to all workshops employing under fifty persons.

1871   Bank Holiday Act passed ... workers' first and only paid holidays

1875   Practice of sending small boys up chimneys to sweep them is banned

1878   Factory Act consolidated all previous Factory Acts into a Factory Code applying to all trades. No child under 10 to be employed. Women not to be employed within four weeks of confinement after childbirth.

1901   Factory and Workshop Act minimum working age raised to 12.

Trade Unions and Strikes

1832   Two strikes of women for equal pay by Yorkshire card setters and at Owen's labour exchange

1833   Women Power Loom Weavers in Glasgow strike for equal pay

1834   Tolpuddle Martyrs

1834   Grand National Consolidated Trades Union, demanded equal pay for women

1835   Female mill workers strike for equal pay

1868   First TUC congress

1874   Women's Protective and Provident League founded

1875   Weavers' strikes in Batley and Dewsbury

1883   Co-operative Women's Guild formed

1888   Women's Trade Union League founded by Clementina Black

1888   Clementina Black moves first successful equal pay resolution at TUC Congress

1875   Strike of Yorkshire weavers led by an all-female strike committee

1888   Matchbox girls' strike in London which paves way for the gas and dock workers' strike

1889   Gas workers' and London dock workers' strike

1906   National Federation of Women Workers founded

Living conditions

1834   The Poor Law Amendment Act passed

1842   First peacetime income tax levied at 7*d* in the pound with a £150 threshold

1846   Repeal of the Corn Laws

1848   First Public Health Act to improve urban conditions, water supplies, sanitary matters

1850s – 1920s Rational Dress Movement

1872   Second Public Health Act ... established sanitary authorities in all areas

1875   Third Public Health Act ... all houses to be connected to water supplies and sewage system

1870s – 1880s network of sewers dug and water pipes laid; gas lighting becomes common

Education

1870   Elementary Education Act provides State education for infants and children aged 5–13

1880   Education Act provides compulsory education for children under 10

1899   Education Act raises age of compulsory education for children to 12

1918   Education Act raises age of compulsory education for children to 14

Bibliography

Bamford, Samuel, *Passages in the Life of a Radical* (1842)

Bamford, Samuel, *Early Days* (1849)

Black Dwarf 1817–1824

Bruton, F.A., *The Story of Peterloo* written for the centenary 16 August 1919 (1919)

Busby, Nicole and Zahn, Rebecca, *A Dangerous Combination* (2016)

Bush, Michael, *The Casualties of Peterloo* (Carnegie 2005)

Dewsbury News 1875

Dictionary of National Biography

Engels, Friedrich, *Condition of the Working Class in England* (1844)

Frow, Edmund and Ruth, *Political Women 1800–1850* (1989)

Hawksley, Lucinda, *March, Women, March* (2013)

Huddersfield Examiner 1875

Lancaster Gazette 1819

Leeds Mercury 1819

Manchester Comet 1822 (Chethams)

Manchester Courier 1819

Manchester Guardian 1820

Manchester Observer 1819–1820

Nadin, Ruth, *Peterloo Massacre* (2008)

Northern Star 1818 and 1843

Oldham Chronicle 1884

Oldham Historical Association (various items)

People's History Museum (various items)

Poole, Robert, *The English Uprising: Peterloo* (Oxford 2019)

Poole, Robert, (ed.) 'Return to Peterloo' (*Manchester Region History Review* volume 23 2012)

Shelley, Percy Byshhe, 'Masque of Anarchy' (written 1819; published
    early 1830s)
The Times 1819 and 1842–3

Websites
www.britishnewspaperarchive.co.uk
www.nationalarchives.gov.uk
www.redflagwalks.wordpress.com
www.spartacus-educational.com

Index